# Young Writers

# Spellbound

## NORTHERN KENT

Poetry Now
Young Writers

Edited by Dave Thomas

First published in Great Britain in 1998 by
*POETRY NOW YOUNG WRITERS*
1-2 Wainman Road, Woodston,
Peterborough, PE2 7BU
Telephone (01733) 230748

HB ISBN 1 86188 844 9
SB ISBN 1 86188 849 X

# FOREWORD

In this, our 5th competition year, we are proud to present *Spellbound Northern Kent.* This anthology represents the very best endeavours of the children from this region.

The standard of entries was high, which made the task of editing a difficult one, but nonetheless enjoyable. The variety of subject matter, creativity and imagination never ceases to amaze and is indeed an inspiration to us all.

This year's competition attracted the highest entry ever - over 46,000 from all over the UK, and for the first time included entries from English speaking children living abroad.

Congratulations to all the writers published in *Spellbound Northern Kent.* We hope you enjoy reading the poems and that your success will inspire you to continue writing in the future.

# CONTENTS

Chatham Grammar School For Girls

| | |
|---|---|
| Donna Hayward | 81 |
| Laura Taylor | 81 |
| Danielle Devereux | 81 |
| Angela Hammond | 82 |
| Leyna Mendham | 82 |
| Anisha Paddam | 83 |
| Shelley King | 84 |
| Lisa Bedelle | 85 |
| Beckie Ferguson | 86 |
| Samantha James | 86 |
| Stacey Bell | 87 |
| Pamela Coothen | 87 |
| Lisa Woollett | 88 |
| Charlotte Jessup | 88 |
| Hayley Usmar | 89 |
| Charlotte Hicks | 90 |
| Nicola Mayes | 91 |
| Katherine Read | 92 |
| Sarah Ayling | 92 |
| Jenna Oliver | 93 |
| Kelly Horan | 94 |
| Amy Adams | 94 |
| Carla O'Hagan | 95 |
| Paula Cross | 96 |
| Vicki Smith | 96 |
| Angela Duffett | 97 |
| Katie-Jayne Alston | 98 |
| Charlotte Pattenden | 99 |
| Suzanne Pert | 100 |
| Sarah Hodge | 100 |
| Niamh Mahon | 101 |
| Rebecca Metcalf | 102 |
| Danielle Sussex | 102 |
| Adelle Walsh | 103 |
| Alice Johnson | 104 |
| Kailey Guest | 105 |
| Joanne Ware | 106 |
| Kerry Prescott | 107 |

# THE POEMS

## UNTITLED

People white
People red
I heard one night
Somebody said
Ten thousand people all in a row
Where does one go?

Some people say your spirits go up to see God,
If you have been good He gives you a nod,
You go up into the golden city,
Where everyone is kind and pretty,

However, if He shakes his head,
You go down to hell instead,
The devil will meet you with a proud grin,
'You're another one who's full of sin'
You go into the dirty city,
Where everyone is horrid and gritty.

So where do *you* go?
The golden city,
Or the gritty city,
Be good and faithful
Then you're all right
And don't forget to say your prayers at night.

*Joy Stockton  (12)*

## WHEN I AM OLD

When I am old I shall ride
a motorbike,
I shall eat dead worms and
all the sweets I like.
I shall put my false teeth on
people's chairs,
And stick chewed up toffees
in their hair.
I shall eat my food from paper
plates,
And ride on swings and roller
skates.
I'll stay up late and dance all
night,
And go to raves, I think I might.
I'll act real mad and go really
wild,
I'll go back to being just like
a child.
I'll do exactly as I please,
'Cause when I'm old I will
be free!

*Carly Hughes (12)*
*Axton Chase School*

## TILLY, MY FRIEND

I have a little friend,
She is black and white,
And nothing at all will end
Our friendship that's holding tight.

I call her 'Little Tilly,'
And when she plays a game
She is really silly,
But I love her all the same.

Tilly is very sweet,
She loves to chase the birds,
Loves to hear them tweet,
And I love her beyond your words.

I wouldn't harm 'Little Tilly',
How could I anyway,
She is really pretty
Every week and every day.

There's one thing for sure,
Tilly's the best I know,
You can only love her more,
And it will always, always show.

*Emma Crabb (12)*
*Axton Chase School*

# NINA

My name is Nina and I like to write,
But it is quite a terrible sight,
Because I can't spell very well.
The writing is not very neat,
So the pages end up in a heap!

*Nina Larkins  (12)*
*Axton Chase School*


# SISTERS

I have a sister,
Much younger than me,
I have a sister
That quarrels with me.

When I'm doing my homework,
And when I'm upstairs,
When I'm eating my lunch,
When I'm saying my prayers

She is there in the daytime
She is there in the night,
She is always there with me,
She is really a fright.

Maybe I'll hate her,
Maybe I can't,
Maybe I'll like her,
Maybe I shan't.

*Amy Jordan  (11)*
*Axton Chase School*

## THE WINDOW

Through that window,
I can see young children playing,
Like ants scurrying -
Ring-a-ring-a-roses,
Is what I hear them saying.

Through that window,
I can see an old people's home,
If I went in, on they would drone,
I can imagine the OAPs sitting, knitting.

Through that window,
I can see a car,
I can hear another from afar,
I can see the car is shiny and new,
I can see a bird as over it flew.

Through that window,
I can see a door,
I am wishing it to open,
So I can seem more,
It opens wide,
Now I can see far inside.

Through that door,
I can see a high flying
Bumble bee,
I have grown to love my garden,
Now I'm old, I suppose it will have to be sold.

Through that door,
I can see no more,
Just the weeds covering the floor.
Just the moss treating the garden
Like it's boss.

*Leonie Wilson  (12)*
*Axton Chase School*

## WHY DOESN'T IT SNOW?

Why doesn't it snow?
It's the middle of winter, isn't it?
When is it going to snow?
How else can I make
Snowballs and snowmen,
Slide down hills on sledges.
It's not fair, is it?
Soon it will be spring,
Then it'll just be hot and
hot for months.
Can't you tell me.

Why doesn't it snow?

*Vanessa Woolf (13)*
*Axton Chase School*


## SPIDERS

I love spiders a whole lot,
I like to cook them in a pot.

It does not matter about their size
I like to take out all their eyes.

I like to pull off all their skin and
use them to put things in.

I like to pull off all their legs
and use them as clothes pegs.

It's not my fault I like insects to eat
I'm just not very keen on meat.

*Sarah Burkett (13)*
*Axton Chase School*

## TIME

What is time
Why is there time
Who made time

Who says that a day starts
When the sun comes up
and ends when it goes down.

Who says that a week
starts on Monday and
ends on Sunday.

What is time.

We all rush around in the
space of time trying to
beat it at its own game
but why.

What is time

Why does time govern
our lives

Time is our greatest enemy

Why is there time

It's killing us all the time.

*Nicholas Stone  (12)*
*Axton Chase School*

## THE SEA

The sea is so beautiful.
Waves splash against the rocks.
White foam makes its way to the beach.
Sea animals roam around inside it.
Children laugh and play around it.
The sea is so beautiful why do
people hurt it.
Sewage is in it.
Dirt and oil splash with the waves
against the rocks.
Black foam makes its way to the beach.
Sea animals getting killed.
Children getting hurt.
The sea is so beautiful why do
people hurt it.

*Louise Nicholls  (13)*
*Axton Chase School*

## SUPER GIRL

I wish that I was Super Girl,
With clothes that change within a twirl,
I'd fly to get a better view,
Of pop stars at a rave review.

Money for friends and old folks too,
Making sure they're never blue,
Homework finished in a flash,
Like washing up and clearing trash.

Princes queuing for a date,
Not sloppy ones or boys I hate,
Live in a big posh country estate,
With rabbits playing by its gate.

I'd spend my life as best I could,
Helping others as you should,
Happiness my one reward,
If I could own a magic sword.

*Jane Keirle  (12)*
*Axton Chase School*


## THE BAD BOYS!

The little boys are very sad
They're sent to bed
Because they were bad
I'm sure it was an accident
But that we'll never know
of how they broke the window
of poor old Mrs Snow
Jack denied it was him
but blamed it on mate Jim
It's all your fault
We can be sure
for kicking the ball
against her door
She will make you pay a fine
for doing that awful crime.

*Emma Pittman  (13)*
*Axton Chase School*

# THROUGH THAT WINDOW

Through that window,
Is a floor made of stone,
The old gate falling to pieces,
and the old ladies across the road,
they chitter, chatter all day long,
Through that window,
There is a little garden,
The lawn is cut,
especially for you
Through that window,
Through those houses,
I see a building site,
builders work all day long,
To try and get these houses done.
Through that window,
I see a school,
It's playtime!
You can see the children playing in the field,
When it snows you see them having snow fights.
Through that window,
There is a park,
I see the children playing,
You can hear screaming football players,
That's all you hear.
Through that window,
I see a bridge,
full of golden lights,
As the cars go by,
It looks so high.

*Rachael Rudland  (12)*
*Axton Chase School*

## MAN U V IPSWICH

The players walked out,
Onto the pitch,
For the cup final,
Man U v Ipswich.

The sun blazed down,
On the Wembley field
Cantona up front,
Keano midfield.

The game kicked off,
The ref started the watch,
Giggs ran down the wing,
He looked at his feet,
There was no ball,
So he did nothing.

Man U scored,
They went 1-0 up,
It was one step further,
To the cup.

At the end of the game,
1-0 was enough,
But the game was scrappy,
The game was rough.

The players went home,
Some happy, some sad,
A 1-0 victory,
But the game was bad.

*Alex Wilson  &  Derek Townshend  (12)*
*Axton Chase School*

## THROUGH THAT HOLE

Through that hole
I can see
A country blooming
Full of trees.

Through that hole
I can see
A light blue sky
Such a pretty blue

Through that hole
I can see
People smiling
People laughing
Not like me.

Through that hole
I can see
In the distance
The wavy sea.

Through that hole
I can see
Brightly coloured flowers
That appeal to me.

Through that hole
I can see
Open spaces
People free.

Something that seems,
Like a dream to me.
But it will be a dream,
Until I'm set free,
Out of this room, by mum.

*Lisa Gotts  (12)*
*Axton Chase School*


## AUTUMN

In the autumn
the air turns cold,
The leaves on the trees,
turn from green to gold.

In the mornings,
there's a carpet of dew,
glistening on plants,
as the sun breaks through.

During the day,
the wind begins to roar,
The sky clouds over,
and rain starts to pour.

In the evenings,
it's wet on the ground,
street lamps come on early,
as cars splash around.

During the night,
the temperature drops,
but I'm in my bed,
where it's cosy and hot.

*Tricia Scott  (12)*
*Axton Chase School*

## COUNTDOWN TO CHRISTMAS

It's started already,
The countdown to Christmas,
Christmas catalogues are in the shops,
People are buying lots of socks,
Christmas dinners are being booked,
Christmas dinners are being cooked,
Christmas lists are being written,
Dolls and teddies and a sweet little kitten.

Now it's time for Hallowe'en,
With witches and pumpkins,
Tricks and treats,
Lots of yummy things to eat.

Bonfire night here we come,
Sparklers, rockets, Catherine wheel
Sausages and potato peel.

The nights draw in,
We change the clocks,
Put on warm undies,
And double socks.

The air is crisp,
The heating on,
The summer heat has
Long since gone.

It's here, Christmas, at last!
Christmas shopping is now in the past,
Excited children can't get to sleep,
Loud carol singers in the street

The turkey's cooking, the stockings are hung,
Time for a rest for poor old mum,
The countdown is over.

*Gemma King  (13)*
*Axton Chase School*


## WORLD AND WHAT I THINK!

Environmentally friendly, that's what we
should be.
Not cutting down,
all of our lovely trees.
We should all be helping
to fight against disease.
We should all be helping.
Please, please, please.

We should not pollute our rivers,
lakes or great big seas,
and we should all be eating,
organics, like green peas.

If we keep on cutting down trees,
there may not be any fresh air to
breathe.
Not only no clean air to breathe,
but may not be even a gentle breeze!

This is just some of the things
that turn this world into that
greenhouse thing.

We can help by picking up litter
instead of being really bitter!

*Lorna Mann  (13)*
*Axton Chase School*

## SCHOOL

School, school, boring school
We haven't even got a swimming pool.
Break times are so short with nothing to do.
We only have time to go to the loo.

Detentions every lunch time how boring can it be.
It's always a shame because
It's always me.

Dinners are gross
You always get peas
Or cold, dry rice and a slice of hard cheese.

Homework every night
Due in the next day.
Teachers say 'take good care I
want it for display'

Last lesson comes , great
It's time to go home.
I've got to do all my homework.
Groan, groan, groan,
Then I spend the rest of the evening
Talking to Kate on the phone.

Although it's good to talk says
Good old BT, my mum and dad
Don't seem to agree.

*Michala Goodwin & Carrie Grainer (12)*
*Axton Chase School*

## WINTER'S DAYS ARE . . .

Winter's days are gloomy and glum,
Winter's days are not much fun.

Winter's days are cold and wet,
Winter's days are chilly and windy.

Winter's days are snowy all day,
Winter's days are where the snowman will stay.

Winter's night has turned to Christmas Day,
Winter's days are fun, real fun!

*Charlotte Furze  (12)*
*Axton Chase School*


## ENDANGERED SPECIES

Ladies and gentlemen, if you want to be included in the auction,
come now,
Our first lot is a Persian cow.
These are endangered species, you may agree,
but please vote because of me.
Our second lot is a Muskrat - I assure you it's no relation to
the vampire bat.
Someone please bid. Please bid even only pounds ten
for this very rare hen.
It's not my fault that the animals are caught and bought.
Someone please buy -
Oh, there's a bid from cousin Jon,
How much do you bid?
Ten pounds you say?
Okay then,
Going . . . going . . . gone!

*Christopher Parkes  (14)*
*Axton Chase School*

# A WALK CAN CLEAR A STEAMY HEAD

As I walk,
I do not talk.
The only sound;
Is my feet covering,
The crunching ground.

As I walk,
My eyes fill with tears.
Just last year;
I wouldn't be on my own.
I wouldn't be walking alone.

As I walk away,
I think I could walk all day.
On the crisp ground,
My feet make a crunchy sound.

As I walk,
I say,
Why did he go away?
Why did he leave me;
To this very day?

As I walk,
I say.
Horses canter,
Mice scamper,
But I just walk away.

*Alice Dean  (12)*
*Axton Chase School*

# THE DOVE FROM ABOVE

Great big fields full of grass,
I can see them from above,
I have big wings and a spotted back,
I found out I'm a dove.

I made my home in a tree,
It was quite a big nest,
I'm getting ready for the snow,
To make the big flight west.

I'm heading for America,
The flight is very long,
I got half way over the ocean,
Then found out I was wrong.

I should have been flying south,
Down to the African coast,
I stopped in a garden on the way,
They chucked me out some toast.

I flew over Nigeria,
I was very full of fear,
A man ran out the jungle,
And stabbed me with his spear.

I never got to Cape Town,
Because I was bleeding and so tired,
I tried to stop the bleeding,
But I couldn't so I died.

So I'm speaking to you from heaven,
Where I rejoined some old friends,
And I send this message down to you
To say that life never ends.

*Christopher Andrews  (12)*
*Axton Chase School*

# A JOY TO KEEP

Ten tiny toes, ten tiny fingers
A mop of ginger hair
A little bundle of joy to keep, to look with such care
And now she's home to keep so warm
and fed and nursed and bathed
I like it when she turns to me and gives a little laugh.
And how she crawls even so small
and now she walks across the hall.
And when she laughs that little smile
you cradle her and she now sleeps
Quietly in slumber deep and then she wakes and up you get
to greet her with your smile.
You hold her tight she sits up now
and feeds herself and messes up her chair
She splats the food upon the floor and stares at you
for comfort and all I do is glare
but she knows your smiling face will soon be there
so funny and you blow upon her little tummy.
She chuckles sweet and grabs her feet she now can reach
that far and picks up things and launches them across the
kitchen floor.
How time flies and how she's grown up so fast, so quick.
And how you wish she was so small with oh so tiny feet.
But now she's older and not so small and off to school
she proudly goes and waves with goodbye kiss.
Out she comes with her beautiful smile
and greets you with a cuddle
A schoolgirl now and growing fast
and soon to be an adult.

*Katie Gibbs  (13)*
*Axton Chase School*

## MY DAD

My dad cooked us dinner
He thinks we are growing thinner
I could hear pots and pans
He thinks he is good with his hands.
It tasted kind of musty
It made me feel rusty.
I'll never let him cook again
He should have been on
'You've Been Framed'.

*Vicky Young  (13)*
*Axton Chase School*


### ROCKET

You
can fire
a firework
where you like.
They fly to a great
height, please
don't set my
hair alight
unless you
want a fight.
They explode
in colours red,
green and blue
and shades
of every hue.

*Matthew Hunt  (12)*
*Axton Chase School*

## SCHOOL

School is so boring you have to
get up at 7 every morning.

Then you have to walk to the
shop and wait at the bus stop.

Then you meet your friends
and get stuck in a conversation.
Which makes you rush to
your first registration.

The first lesson is a doss with
that boy behind with the
smoker's cough.

Next lesson is maths with multiplication
then English with all that punctuation.

I can't wait till break and
get some food
the boy behind trumped, 'Oh Jim
you're so rude.'

The boys in the playground were
having a fight
about a stupid argument they
had last night.

The teacher came over full of
tension
and gave them both a few days
suspension.

Then we had 2 more lessons
which were full of depression.

Then home time came until
tomorrow it starts again.

*Katy Fairman (14)*
*Axton Chase School*

## DIFFERENT

Why is it wrong to be different?
Why do they stop and stare?
Are they noisy or thick or concerned?
Or is it they just don't care?

We didn't choose to be different.
It just sort of happened that way.
Why can't they accept us for who we are?
Because that's the way we will stay.

Their words can be mean or hurtful or worse.
They don't understand what they're saying.
It's not always easy to follow the trend.
The trend that society's laying.

I'm not saying we should be ignored.
Just to be treated the same.
We have feelings like everyone.
So don't treat us like we're to blame.

*Sarah Cunnington (12)*
*Axton Chase School*

## WHEN I WAS A BABY

When I was a baby I was a right pain.
I wasn't satisfied with a teddy or a toy train
I cried nearly every minute of the day,
until at last I got my own way.

I used to have one of those pull back cars
Which I loved so much because it went so far
But one day I lost it through a hole in the wall,
So then I had to play with my shiny red ball.

I cried and cried all night long
unless my mother sang me a song
and when she did it would be 'Rock-a-bye Baby'
Because she was really a very nice lady.

*Nadine Jewell  (12)*
*Axton Chase School*

## POEM OF THE WORLD

The world, what has happened to it?
The world, more polluted every minute,
The world, why is it there?
The world, has buildings everywhere.

The world, why am I here?
The world, my family are near,
The world, green and blue,
The world, me and you.

The world, surviving is tough,
The world, some people live rough,
The world, with plants and trees,
The world, oceans and seas.

The world, too much crime,
The world, not enough time.

*David Flack  (13)*
*Axton Chase School*


## GUESS

Waiting, waiting, waiting for something
Exciting to happen.
Suddenly I am being picked up and being taken
Through a mysterious dark tunnel.
Look I can see a tiny slither of light
I'm getting closer and closer.
I'm in daylight, thousands of funny looking
Humans are screaming and shouting.
I've been put down on a firm and hard ground.
Something's moving towards me very fast
Please somebody *Save me!*
A foot with a lot of spikes is coming
Towards me.
*Ouch, ouch, eekk!* What's happening to me.
I'm making a hissing noise as if a snake
Has just arrived from the desert.
I'm shrinking fast, I'm getting smaller, help me
*Pssssttttt.*

I am a football!

*Nicholas King  (11)*
*Borden Grammar School*

## THE DAY I DECIDE

It sits in the garage filthy dirty.
I know it wants to get out, I can feel it
Urging me to let it out
I wish I could help it
I really do
But I can't.

Day after day I go out there and see it sitting there,
Wishing for me to let it out,
I wish I could help it,
I just can't.

Then one day I decide 'enough is enough'
I take the garage keys and away I go
I give it a kick and a good old twist,
and we ride off together

Just me and my motor cycle.

*Daniel Howard  (11)*
*Borden Grammar School*


## WITHOUT YOU

This is the way it's got to be,
Sat on a pew with a picture of you,
Praying that I'll see you again,
There must be more to life than this.

Sitting in hope that I'll be able to cope,
And wait another year, but still I fear,
There's just a chance,
I'll never see your smile again.

Your magnet eyes have drawn me in.
You'll never know how far I'll go,
To make sure you're unspoiled.
Why won't you tell me what you're thinking?

I cry for you, I'd die for you,
But friends is all we stay, I need to get away.
I must escape this town,
Life without you is getting me down.

*Phillip Simpson  (14)*
*Borden Grammar School*


## SCHOOL CUSTARD

Squidgy, squelchy, bubbly, belchy,
Squashy, boshy, mushy, sloshy,
Why is it given to me?

Burgling, gurgling,
My stomach keeps churning,
Oozing, groozing,
My appetites losing,
Can't they find something good to eat,
Like cherries, strawberries or even sweets!

I can't eat it,
I can't.

Squidgy, squelchy, bubbly, belchy.
Squashy, boshy, mushy, sloshy,
Why is it given to me?

*Thomas Merriman  (11)*
*Borden Grammar School*

## DIFFERENCES

I go high, you go low.
I go fast, you go slow.
I rotate, you rock.
I go in the net, you go somewhere wet
I'm leather, you're rock-hard.
I fly, you stay on the ground
I bounce, you just land.
I'm round, we have no hands.
We have a shell, I hear a bell
I also go bang, you don't.
I get kicked, you don't
I am a football and you're a plain
tortoise.

*Steven Baxendale  (11)*
*Borden Grammar School*


## MORNING SOUNDS

It wakes you in the morning
With a sharp burst of sound
It stops you in the morning from lying around.

It wakes you up at dawn
As you get up you yawn
You see the sight of sunlight
Now you've woken up all bright.

You wake up to the sound alert
You get up and pull on your shirt.

As you wake with a shock
You should know by now it's an alarm clock.

*David Taylor  (11)*
*Borden Grammar School*

## DEADLY SCHOOL DINNERS

These are the graves of the three poor sinners,
Who died after eating the Borden school dinners,
The meat's made of iron,
The spuds are of steel,
If that doesn't kill you,
*The pudding will!*

Lumpy custard,
Mouldy peas,
Black fish fingers,
Rotting cheese.

These are some things,
God didn't intend,
We'll have to slay the cook,
Unless he makes amends.

But the cook always escapes,
And runs down his drive,
We all chase after him,
And he comes out with a knife!

I whipped out some machine guns,
There's no more of his cruel species,
I paid the undertaker to write,
On his tombstone . . .

*Rest in pieces!*

*Antony Willis  (11)*
*Borden Grammar School*

# RIDDLE-ME-REE

*Code breaker* 1 to 26
  A to Z

Firstly we'll start with a clue;
I am made of paper
My first letter is in 1 x 2,
My second letter is in 3 x 5,
My third letter is in 50 - 35,
Guessed yet . . . come on!
My final letter is in 15 - 4,
Have you got the answer,
That's it, *Book!*

Here is the clue,
I am protective clothing
My first letter is in 150 - 149
My second letter is in 9 x 2
Have you guessed?
My third letter is in 10 + 5 - 2
My fourth letter is in 10 x 2 ÷ 5
Come on, you should have guessed?
My fifth letter is in 10 x 2 x 0 +1
My final letter is in 9 x 9 - 80 + 17
You've guessed the answer now,
That's right *Armour!*

***James Harland (11)***
***Borden Grammar School***

# BUILDING BRIDGES

You can build a bridge out of
bricks and stone,
You can build a bridge out of
wood.
But to build a bridge out of
two enemies, is harder than
it should.

To make a final decision,
To be fair both sides.
Even when there's two different minds.

You can build a bridge out of
bricks and stones,
You can build a bridge out of
wood.
But to build a bridge out of
two enemies, is harder than it
should.

You try to please two people,
But end up pleasing one,
Oh, I wish they would start having fun.

You can build a bridge out of
bricks and stones,
You can build a bridge out of
wood,
But to build a bridge out of
two enemies, is harder than
it should.

*Christopher Rabey (11)*
*Borden Grammar School*

## THE BEAUTY OF THE WORLD

As morning breaks there is only one sound
Piercing the silence, it is that of
The dawn chorus the beauty of the songs
Are sounds of affection to each other
The birds flutter away as the
Sun rises and the glorious morning begins.
As the day grows on the
Light crashes through the trees,
There is a loud shriek and then
Silence, it is now that the beauty
Of the world is shattered and the
Forest is once again in darkness.

*Jonathan Thompson  (11)*
*Borden Grammar School*


## THIS LIFE

I'll squash that fly and it'll go splat,
I can't be bothered with school and all that.
When I get home from school I kick off my shoes,
And get a big case of the homework blues.
Eating is what I like doing best,
Watching the box and having a rest,
Scoffing biscuits and downing tea,
That's got to be the life for me.
The rest of the time it's all doom and gloom,
'Cause Mum says I've got to tidy my room.
I pick up my clothes and shove them in a drawer,
                              till I can't fit anymore.
I've squashed that fly and it did go *splat!*

*Gary Nash  (15)*
*Borden Grammar School*

## I'M TIRED OF LIFE - WHAT CAN I DO?

I am iron.
I don't like the black powder.
It makes me want to sneeze.
I'm old now.
I'm rusting to bits now.
I'm tired of doing nothing.
The black powder is still there.
I like fire,
But I don't like it when there is a big fire though.
I'm so stressed, tired of life.
I'm lonely.
What can I do?

***Colin Broadbridge  (11)***
***Borden Grammar School***


## WHAT AM I

I'm man's best friend,
I can twist and bend
I'm black and white,
I'll give you a fright.
If you want to buy me I'm 30p.
I'm large and thin,
I won't make a din,
I'll hold your fish and chips,
Or kebab instead.
Put me in water and I'll be dead,
Because even I can't do the backstroke!
So, what do you think I am?
Yes that's right a . . .

       Newspaper!

***Gavin Skinner  (11)***
***Borden Grammar School***

# FRANCE

France is a wonderful country,
With the Pyrenees along the south
And the Alps all along the east.

In the south there are lovely beaches
Over the Pyrenees is Spain
Over to the north-east is Belgium

On a ferry heading for England,
In a car going to Italy
Or just somewhere in France itself.

In Paris there's the Eiffel Tower,
The Louvre and the Arc de Triomphe
And also a river, the Seine

There's Austria nearby for skiing
And Spain is near for the sun
But France is nice for holidays too.

*Scott Vaughan  (11)*
*Borden Grammar School*


# A DAY

It's morning
Everyone wakes up
Shops start to open
Greengrocers the lot.

I see everything happen
Way up high
I see everybody
Saying goodbye.

In the afternoon
The children leave school
I see all the people
Saying hello.

It's night-time
The lights are turned off
All of the people
Are saying goodnight.

***Christopher Dean  (11)***
***Borden Grammar School***


## THE GREAT VIEW OF THE GAME

I'm an object that gets hit a lot
If the bowler has a good shot
I'm a set of three
Cut from a tree

There is a strange man throwing something
When it hits me I go *Ping!*
When this happens a man goes off
And then another man comes on with a cough.

The day goes on
Until the sun has gone
My two friends keep me warm
We stay together until dawn.

But we don't mind, we don't need tickets
Because we are the wickets!

***Oliver Mundy  (11)***
***Borden Grammar School***

## FALCONS

Peregrine falcons are tiny colourful hunters,
They circle around the clouds and swoop.
They turn into a streak of colour,
Diving at the white dove below them,
Their talons lock and they spin to earth,
The falcon lets go at the last minute,
His prey is ready for eating.

*Adam Stratford  (11)*
*Borden Grammar School*


## THE AQUATIC ANIMAL

I'm swift and sleek
My tail beats true
I'm an aquatic animal
Water I swim through.

My tail is stiff and is not multicoloured
I don't have gills and scales
Yet I swim through the water with grace and ease.

My fur is black as the night in the water
Yet when I get out it is a dull brown.

I swim with Neptune the god of the sea
He takes me on tours around his palace
Yet I'm still back for tea.

Guess what I am you humans you?
One little clue, you see me in a zoo.

*I am an otter.*

*Philip Broadbridge  (11)*
*Borden Grammar School*

## HE WAS ALONE

The boy stood there very quietly.
A large grey mass stood there,
With children chattering.
But he wouldn't know,
He was alone,
Spellbound.

Open gaps and shutters,
Cars whizzed behind.
People endeavoured to get his attention.
But he wouldn't know,
He was alone,
Spellbound.

Older children moved by him,
All smartly dressed,
All looking clean.
But he wouldn't know,
He was alone,
Spellbound.

'Shouldn't you be in?'
The boy awoke, 'What?'
'Hurry along now.'
He entered the mass,
(A senior school),
Spellbound.

*Nicholas Evans (13)*
*Borden Grammar School*

## SUPER SPURS

Tottenham, come on, give it all you've got,
Come on Armstrong, have a shot.
Andy Sinton to Ruel Fox with a cross
Ferdinand in the area waiting to nod it in
Down the other end it's Walker with a kick
Ferdie volleys it on and looks really slick
Gerry Francis he's the Tottenham boss,
When they lose he is very cross.

*Miles Maclaren (11)*
*Borden Grammar School*


## BLUE

Blue is a cool, calm colour
Resembled by a bluebell flower.

Blue is the colour of the sea
The wind the rain and the sky
Is blue your favourite colour?
Why?

Blue is the colour for a beautiful
Baby boy, your favourite colour jeans
or your most wonderful toy.

Blue is the colour of lips
When cold outside
Is blue your favourite colour?
You decide.

*Sam Adams (15)*
*Borden Grammar School*

## 90'S KIDS

Drinking the night away,
young kids come out to play,
12, 11, 10, they don't care,
older people just look and stare.

After dark they come out to fight,
Fridays, Saturdays, sometimes a school night,
What would their parents say and do,
if they found out what they got up to.

'Not that one Mum it's got a hood,
I'll get beaten up believe me I would.'
            'Nonsense, son, it's really nice,
            and look it's even a decent price.'
'Shut up Mum you haven't a clue,
and look it's even a girlie light blue.'
            'Then maybe you'll like this one in red?'
            'Get real Mum I wouldn't be seen in it dead.'

Night-time comes and they're all out again,
John, Paul, Sammy, Richard and Ben,
it's gone past 12 and some older kids come,
John, Paul, Sammy, Richard and Ben start to run,
John's got the booze and Paul's got the fags,
Ben's got the white powder in the little plastic bags,
John says 'Where's Sammy, where did he run?'
Richard says 'I bet that chicken's gone back to his Mum.'
But Sammy's been caught and is getting kicked in,
and then left for dead beside a little green bin,
his Mum goes mad because she thinks he is dead,
but none of this would have happened if he'd been
                                    good instead.

*Gareth Collins  (14)*
*Borden Grammar School*

# THE MAN OF MANY COLOURS

An old man who drank coffee
(It was bad for him, he knew)
Was also addicted to toffee
In the end his teeth turned blue

He never bought any gold rings
(Because he was very mean)
Instead he bought only brass things
So his fingers turned dark green

For breakfast he ate cold beans
(He never got out of bed)
He's been like that since his teens
And so his hair turned red

He wanted to wash his hair
(Or that is what you might think)
But in fact he washed his chair
And all the wood turned bright pink

With apples he liked to have custard
(And he always wore his mac)
But sometimes he liked having mustard
And so all his toes turned black

He always like to eat late
(But never had enough light)
And so he put bulbs on his plate
And painted all his coal white

He took his dog to the vet
(Then said that he wouldn't pay)
And so got another pet
And then sprayed his tortoise grey

He caught a cold in his house
(And when he went into town)
He came back with a dead mouse
And all the snow turned brown.

*Gavin Alexander  (13)*
*Borden Grammar School*


# SEASONS OF THE YEAR

Summer has gone,
Leaves turn brown.
Autumn approaching,
Leaves falling down.

Trees are now bare,
Leaves form a mound,
Winter approaching
Frost on the ground.

Snow in the air,
So silent and white.
Winter is here now,
With spring not in sight.

Shoots start appearing,
New life has begun.
Bulbs come alive,
With the warm spring sun.

Colourful flowers,
The heat of the day.
Summer is with us,
I hear you say.

*Stuart Roberts  (14)*
*Borden Grammar School*

## WINTER DAYS

Jewelled grass over the land,
Crisp brunette leaves,
Hazelnuts,
Chestnuts plunge with a fracture,
Children throwing snowballs,
Pictures in the warmed steamed up windows,
People tobogganing down the white sheet of snow,
Red faces of ecstatic, delighted children,
Reflections off the puddles,
The smell of roast stuffed turkey,
Icicles on the roofs of people's dwellings,
Ice drops fissured,
The snowmen looking over fields,
The smell of apple pie,
Christmas puddings take over the scent of the air,
Amazing embellishment in living rooms.

*William Lay (11)*
*Borden Grammar School*


## THOUGHTS ON SPACE

The Universe is gigantic, the Universe is vast,
From galaxy to galaxy, you hop in your spacecraft.
The Russians were the first in space, with their Sputnik 2,
But the Americans landed first, with the first man on the moon.

We observe through a telescope, looking into space,
Hoping to see an alien, with a weird and wonderful face.
What aliens may look like, none of us seem to know,
I have my thoughts and visions, but in my dreams to space I go.

Jupiter is the biggest planet, and Mercury is very small,
But the sun shines over us, big and bright and tall.
Our Universe is infinite, our Universe is unknown,
But of all the places I'd like to be, I'd rather be at home.

*Simon Jones  (14)*
*Borden Grammar School*


## FEAR

Walking through the woods at night
Dark as can be and no company
You hear a noise and are filled with fright
Walking faster, faster, fearing to slow
More noises you hear, 'Who is there?'
The sound comes closer, where to go?
Moving on, hear an almighty crack
As the fear rises, you begin to run
Racing through the trees, too scared to look back
Running and running, trip and fall to the floor
Foot is trapped and in pain
Trying to get up, trying more and more
The noise is getting closer as you get free
Look back and see a figure against the night
Can't make out a face, too dark to see
Look up see a light through the trees, it's home
Going and going, nearly there
Hear more noise, the man is not alone
Get indoors, there's a ringing in your ear
But you know that you're safe
But never again will you feel such fear?

*Thomas Hoggins  (13)*
*Borden Grammar School*

## DEATH

I have many anxieties
About what my life will bring.
Will I be a millionaire?
Or will I learn to sing?

Spiders and darkness
Are just two of my fears.
Will I learn to conquer them?
Or will it end in tears?

This is all a cover-up
For my biggest fear of all,
Which is *death!*

What will happen when I die?
How will I die?
Will I be shot,
By a government spy?

I don't want to be trapped in a box
With nothing to do,
Nowhere to go
And gaze into nothing but an endless void.

What will happen if they get it wrong
And I am, after all, still alive?
I've heard of it happening,
But will I survive?

Will I see a pure light leading into Utopia?
Or will I see a burning flame leading to the
                                    Underworld?
Or maybe I will even be born again?

I should not worry about this
Because it is many years ahead,
But you never know when your time will be up,
And when you will be dead.

*James Henley  (13)*
*Borden Grammar School*


# KIM

*(In memory of my grandparents' dog, Kim)*

A cross-bred collie by the name of Kim,
Crept into the crypt that the cat crept in.
Looked all around and being alone,
Started to dig, and unearthed a bone.

This made Kim's tail wag with glee,
She said 'I'll take it home for tea.'
But on the wall above her head,
Kim spied a plaque, the writing read:
'Here lies the body of William Tree,
Buried in seventeen eighty three.'

Nothing of his life was said,
But simply stated that he was dead.
Well, thought Kim, I can rest assured,
That my next meal will be matured.

So home to tea ran our Kim,
Out of the crypt that the cat crept in,
Down the path, and past the graves,
Under a bush and out the gates.
She did not even dare to stop,
As she had to be back by 5 o'clock.

*Timothy Brissenden  (14)*
*Borden Grammar School*

## THE LIFE OF SOMETHING

*Bang! Bang! Crash! Oh no!*
Something in the trees,
Straying to and fro,
*Bang! Bang! Crash! Oh no!*

Coming, stomping
Ground is shaking
Leaves falling now
Lives are in danger
Now I know
       it's a stranger.

It may be a monster
Really scary
Just like a roller-coaster
I better not cry.
I'd be called a wimp
As well as a blimp
I better flee.
*Oh no! It's got me!*

**Christopher Williams  (11)**
**Borden Grammar School**


## THE CAT

The mighty monstrous cat,
From number twenty eight,
The prodigious annoying cat,
That everyone would hate.

He secretly crawls into your house,
And picks an almighty fight,
With some helpless little mouse,
And kills them all with his might.

The cat, so black and hairy,
With enormous claws,
The cat can get so really lairy,
He cuts you, and scratches you, and loudly roars.

Never get into a fight with this cat,
He will tear you apart,
He will bite you like a smelly rat,
And that is only the start.

*Michael Betts  (14)*
*Borden Grammar School*

## THE SPRINT

Waiting at the start
The most drawn-out ten seconds of your career awaits
You hear the gun
The expectancy is over!
You're out of the blocks
The ten-metre mark is over.
Twenty, thirty, forty, fifty and sixty metres have gone
And you are still behind.
Seventy metres,
You're there or there abouts
Eighty metres,
And here you come.
Ninety metres,
You're almost there as you duck for the line
It's all over as you turn to see the time!
Yes, you have won at 9.09 seconds
You have the *gold*
And your dream.

*Chris Warne  (13)*
*Borden Grammar School*

# A SCARY CHILDHOOD

You shoot out of bed like a rocket,
You start crying a little stream,
Everybody comes and stares at you,
Because of that little dream.

Your parents give you lots of toys,
To make sure you are happy,
You have that scary dream again,
And wet your little nappy.

From under the covers you come,
Your face lights up like a beam,
For once again, you're free,
From that scary little dream.

*Jodie Doubleday  (14)*
*Borden Grammar School*

# FOOTBALL

It's a game with a ball,
And eleven players on each team,
Chasing each other round the pitch,
Listening to the supporters scream.
At the shrill of the whistle the game begins,
The rough and tumble tackling
dispels any grins,
'Pass it up the line' is the
constant battle call,
Racing to see who can catch up
with the bouncing leather ball.
The game is called *football!*

*Tom Godbold  (11)*
*Borden Grammar School*

## No One Cares Anymore

I'm walking around and what do I see?
Lots of rubbish on the floor.
Lots of pollution in the sea.
No one cares anymore.

I'm walking around and what do I do?
I kick a can on the grass,
And see a dog go to the loo,
No one cares anymore.

I'm walking around and what do I think?
I think it's disgusting to see,
A man who has had too much to drink,
No one cares anymore.

I'm walking around and what do I hear?
Kids of my age getting alcohol poisoning,
Drinking spirits and beer,
No one cares anymore.

I'm walking around and what do I see?
Black smoke in the air
It has come out of the factory chimneys,
No one cares anymore.

I'm walking around and what do I become?
I'm friends with the children,
Of the people who are scum,
Who destroy the world for the rest
And *no one cares anymore!*

*Jonathan Spratt  (13)*
*Borden Grammar School*

## HELENA

My little cousin, is almost ten months old,
And now she has learnt to stand up on her feet.
She is getting very bold,
She joined our family on the 14th December,
A day I will always remember,
With her big greeny-blue eyes, and light brown hair,
She really is a beauty beyond compare,
Ten perfect little fingers, ten perfect little toes,
Tiny little lips and a little button nose,
She often talks in baby chatter,
Which I can't understand, but that does not matter,
Whenever I see her she gives me a big smile,
Which means she wants me to play for a while,
She likes to chase me up and down the hall,
She has mastered a very speedy crawl,
I visit her whenever I can,
When we walk into town, I like to push her pram,
She really is a perfect little miss,
It's really cute when she gives me a kiss.

*Daniel James Taroni (14)*
*Borden Grammar School*


## THE HAUNTED HOUSE

The haunted house of Almond Square
All dark and evil, all old and bare,
And if you see it before your bed
The thoughts of this house roll in your head.

It stands where cold winds chill
And where ghosts love to *thrill!*
Step in a puddle, it starts to quiver
You enter the house, your body shivers.

Now you're in the grand old hall,
*How can anyone live here at all?*
But all thoughts stop when you see
The old ghost of King Henry!

You realise this place is no fun,
So you turn your back and start to run
There is a question you need to know,
How far will your imagination go?

***Thomas Holdstock (11)***
***Borden Grammar School***


# THE BOY WENT TO SCHOOL

A boy came into our school
Not worried about the rules,
On his feet he wore trainers
No thoughts of complainers.

Reported to class no collar, no tie,
Smiled and looked teacher straight
in the eye.

The class were all stunned,
And the boy, he was shunned,
Our teacher just smiled,
And said 'Man you look wild.'

The class all said 'Cool'
We'll all break the rules
The teacher just laughed
and then he sat down
That's right he said . . .
        *'They're only for clowns!'*

***Simon Meeks (13)***
***Borden Grammar School***

## LIFE ON THE STREET

Life on the street
Dark and dusty
Rubbish in the gutter
Nobody cares, nobody knows

No money, no food
No home, no life
Always cold, always poor
Nobody cares on a dark damp night.

Begging for money
Trying to get out of the rut
Always seems endless
No end to the torture
I always run out of the luck

Nobody cares what happens to me,
Because my life's on the street.

*Matthew Marchant (15)*
*Borden Grammar School*


## THE FLEA AND THE DOG

My friend Pongo is really snug,
He lets me drink his delicious blood,
He keeps me warm and tight,
Just as a friend should show his might.

Wherever he goes, I go too,
Whenever he stops, I stop too,
Whatever he does, I do too,
But Pongo is my best friend.

He keeps me blissful all year round,
He lets me play with his furry roots,
And explore his bushy boots,
But there's one thing wrong with my friend Pongo.

In winter he's always wet,
So I have to find a brand-new pet,
So now I have a brand-new friend,
Keeping me warm as a friend should be.

*David Steele  (13)*
*Borden Grammar School*

## THE ALPHABET

The alphabet has 26 letters in all,
Some letters are tiny,
Some letters are small,
The letters are split into categories, two,
There are five vowels,
And 21 consonants too.
The alphabet starts with an A, B, C, D,
Continuing with E, F
And ending with Z.
The letters, put together, make hundreds of words,
Like 'playing' and 'looking',
And 'totally absurd'.
These words make up sentences,
Like 'See you, I'm going,'
And I have used letters,
            to make up this poem!

*Michael Lovelock  (14)*
*Borden Grammar School*

## WE ARE THE ANT ARMY

My men are tough
With all their might,
They are so rough
And now they fight.
We *are* the Ant Army.

Now we will strike
As we are mean,
Do as we like
Just don't get seen.
We *are* the Ant Army.

Hurry my men
Now grab the fruit,
Pick up that pen
Take back the loot.
We *are* the Ant Army.

We march to camp
At a great speed,
With loot and lamp
Past the great weed.
We *are* the Ant Army.

Now get some rest
For the next raid,
If you're the best
You will get paid.
You *are* the Ant Army.

*Amrish Patel  (13)*
*Borden Grammar School*

## SPELLBOUND

It was a time of darkness and a time of treason,
A time not enlightened, a time before reason.

He flies in the air as swift as a swallow,
His wings soar through the sunset,
And on into tomorrow.
He appears so bold, the ruler of the night,
His wings so colossal
Which grant him his flight.

And from the darkness of the night
A child's scream breaks the silence.
A sacrifice has taken place
For this being of wisdom and violence.

Slayers approach his wicked cave
Pacing through the debris
This creature did save.
The rule is a person never talks,
Never whispers or never walks
When confronted by a corpse.
So the slayers stood with fear
While a heavy breathing
Blew in one's ear.
That night, five did enter the cave,
But out of them all
Only one did survive.
So from that very time till now
A legend has been foretold,
That if you hear something wicked or foul,
A scent of a dragon or a swift-like sound,
Then go to your homes and lock yourself in
For here comes the almighty *Spellbound.*

*Chris Brodigan  (13)*
*Borden Grammar School*

## TWENTY FOUR HOURS

The most dangerous creature in the wild,
is the mayfly.
A single mayfly,
With a single stare,
can curse a horse to die,
This is a rare occurrence
but the sadistic try,
to maim, or at least, cause offence.
From a leaf it prepares to strike.
It bends and springs . . .
   . . . it loses time and dies.
Mayflies have a poor sense of timing.

*Graeme Broadbridge  (15)*
*Borden Grammar School*


## AN OCCUPATIONAL HAZARD

A doctor, no, a driver I think,
or a goalkeeper like Nigel Spink.
I might drive a BT van,
or be a travelling salesman.

I could learn to play the violin,
perhaps watch over and keep down the din.
A famous actor would be nice,
supervisor in a factory of dice.

I could, I might, become a king,
or do for the world a very special thing.
But as I am still at school,
I will stick to the swimming pool.

Being thirteen is an occupational hazard!

*Sam Bennett  (13)*
*Borden Grammar School*

## THE HAUNTED LIBRARY

I walk in through the almighty doors,
see the never ending books.
Feel an icy chill rush past,
numbing my poor terrified hands.
I feel a sense of abnormality,
as I look down an aisle of first editions,
The musty odour wafts around me
I feel a ghostly tingle about me.
This unearthly feeling makes my hair stand on end.
I hear whispers in the silence,
see eyes glowing in between the books,
staring.
Hear the banging of the doors opening and closing.
A soft patter of ghostly footsteps,
the huge shelves closing in on me,
the footsteps getting closer and closer,
louder and louder.
I start to run,
through the aisles,
faster and faster.
But still the patter catches me.
'Can I help you?'
asks the old twisted librarian.
'Please don't run in the halls.'
Then she disappears into thin air,
and I am left with a loud evil cackle
I head out of the huge doors,
Back into the cool air.
Well away from the library!

*Matthew Probert (12)*
*Borden Grammar School*

## THE ENORMOUSLY POWERFUL HORSE

There was an enormously powerful horse,
He liked to run on his own course.
He always entered competitions,
But only in certain conditions.
He had his favourite saddle,
Which he always groomed with his paddle
On one occasion he had bad luck,
And fell right over a duck.
He was out of the race,
Much to his disgrace.
He left with his tail between his legs,
And flew right over some pegs.
He left the floor,
All the way to the door.
And for this time at least,
He had been beaten by a beast,
So the enormously powerful horse was ceased.

*Chris Steele  (13)*
*Borden Grammar School*

## WANDERING IN THE NIGHT

I scuttled around from side to side
The wind blowing on my spines.
I look up and in the sky
I see the clouds passing by the moon.

As I look about I soon
Notice a tin of old dog food,
I go to eat it but looking gloomy
A dog began to charge at me.

I ran down the path beside the wall
And rolled up into a tight ball,
With my spikes sticking out I knew the mongrel
Would never attempt to attack me.

When I was sure that it had gone
I simply got up and walked away,
For I was tired and needed a place to go
A hedgehog's life is hard you know.

*Matthew Orwin  (11)*
*Borden Grammar School*

## HOMEWORK

Homework
Frustration. Monotony.
Headache.
Football calling.
*Tick, tock, tick, tock!*
Time-consuming
Boredom, tedious
Eight o'clock, Eastenders?
*Tick, tock, tick, tock!*
Difficult questions -
What was that answer?
*Tick, tock, tick, tock!*
Is it teatime?
Was that the doorbell?
*Tick, tock, tick, tock!*
Almost done - phew!
*Tick, tock, tick, tock!*
Finished . . .
. . . Time for bed!

*Alexander Kitney  (11)*
*Borden Grammar School*

## RETIREMENT

The time has come to turn in the towel,
I've been working here for eight years now,
I'm retiring tomorrow,
Much to my disbelief.

There've been some good times
There've been some bad times
There won't be any more,
For I'm turning in the towel tomorrow,
                              much to my disbelief.

I've made lots of friends,
Some good ones at that,
Now I have to leave them
I'll never be back.

I travel to work, to and fro
It takes an hour but I don't care,
I go in my car,
As it's so very far to walk.

I like my work a lot,
I don't want to leave
I don't think I will,
I'm quite happy where I am.

*Andrew Nanson (13)*
*Borden Grammar School*

## FRED'S FEAR

Fred thought he was a pretty nice chap,
Sitting by the fire with a dog on his lap,
But his wife burned his dinner again and again,
He thought he could take it, but suddenly then,
That's when he realised that was the last straw.
So he picked up a knife and struck her to the floor.
He slit and mangled her small throat,
But only the body he took to the boat.
Without his wife's cooking he was finally free,
And he dumped his wife's body into the sea.
Then returned to the house, trembling with fear
And mounted her head - what a strange souvenir!
There was a knock on the door which triggered a thought,
It could be the police and he had been caught.
He looked through the spy hole and shook with fright,
The police had arrived on this night of all nights.
He opened the door and they said with a sigh,
'We've found your wife's body at the end of Lake High.
she was found by a crew repairing the power,
Now they've been shaking for over an hour.
I know it's late, Sir, but before you go to bed,
We observed that the body was minus its head.'
Fred was arrested, convicted and died in a scream
And woke the next morning, it was just a dream.
Fred sat by the fire with a dog on his lap,
But his wife burned the dinner again and again,
Fred shook with horror, it had started again.

*Graham Hart (15)*
*Borden Grammar School*

## THE GREAT GREEN WARRIOR

I am the *Great Green Warrior,*
Tall as a house,
For I am so quiet,
Quiet as a mouse.

I am the *Great Green Warrior,*
With nerves of steel,
My home is high,
High on a hill.

I am the *Great Green Warrior,*
Swaying in the breeze,
I could live here forever,
With some ease.

I am the *Great Green Warrior,*
With high-class,
Well actually I'm a blade of
       grass!

***Aden Philpott (11)***
***Borden Grammar School***


## LIFE TO DEATH

When I walk in shadows,
Shadows so dark.
With gravestones around me,
Birds in the sky.

Why can't I see
Through the shadows so dim?
Leaping and swirling as
Its breath on my cheek so cold.

As people gather around
I look down and I see,
Weeping and wailing,
My body so still.

In the shadows now I can see,
The light that is fading.
What can it be
But death that's coming to me?

*Joe Demian  (14)*
*Borden Grammar School*


## SMOKEY

S  moky is as small as a dwarf,
O  h, how soft he is
F  urry and silky like a pile of soft feathers
T  he long droopy ears and tiny twitching nose
                                    are kind and gentle.

S  mall black eyes, searching around
I   n his cage he chews on his food
L  ying in the hay and sawdust that covers his hutch floor
K  ind and gentle as he hops
Y  ummy, he seems to say as he chews up our lawn.

S  mokey shares his hut with a tiny guinea pig called Holly
M ost of the time they spend together roaming the garden
O  ften he tries to climb into the house and hide
K  indly Smokey never fights with Holly
E  ars drooped Smokey sleeps easily at night
Y  es, of course, my pet is a Dutch dwarf rabbit.

*Darren Searle  (11)*
*Borden Grammar School*

## Pepsi The Cat

At 6am in the morning
Just as the day is dawning
The sun is taking off its hat
Helping to wake our family cat
He wakes and stretches body legs and paws
Swiftly he scratches at the bedroom doors
Who needs a cockerel like the ones on the farm
With Pepsi the cat we have the *purr-fect* alarm.

The noise of the scratching is so rude
Hinting at his need for morning food
Starting his day in his usual way
Leads him on from food to play
Now out to the garden for a good look around
Preying on any little creatures that can be found.

On arrival home from school
He is there to greet me as a rule
He likes to be stroked and for me to fuss
Our family pet Pepsi, the puss.
It really seems the day has gone quick
The cat falls asleep as his final trick.

*James Gibson  (11)*
*Borden Grammar School*


## The Law

It is set as a guideline,
Often it is obeyed,
Often it is broken,
It has to be respected.

It has a purpose,
Merely to help, not hinder,
To protect the innocent,
To deal with the guilty.

By few it is not respected,
If a crime is committed,
Or a person has overstepped the line,
The law is there to be enforced.

*Tim Wood  (15)*
*Borden Grammar School*


## MY MUM'S PET ALIEN

My mum owns a pet alien,
It has medium blondy-brown hair,
And blue eyes.

My mum owns a pet alien,
It's 138cm in height,
And weighs 31kg.

My mum owns a pet alien
She lets it listen to Spice Aliens
And its most captivating read is
                    'Five Children and It'.

My mum owns a pet alien,
It sucks its finger
And carries around a golden-yellow duck.

My mum owns a pet alien,
My mum's pet alien is of course
                    *my sister!*

*Alastair Stringfellow  (12)*
*Borden Grammar School*

## THE RIVER

It goes sluggishly over the flat ground,
And rapidly down the gradient hills,
Then it slows down to a steady pace then
It hits the rocks on the bank,
Sluggishly it enters a competition area.

But what lay ahead, another gradient hill.
It went faster and faster, nearly hit forty knots.
Then once again it hit the rocks and banks,
And then it approached the canoe competition,
And turned into white water rapids.

Up ahead was a resting waterfall,
It flies over the top and hits the water with a big *splash!*
It calms down to a trickle,
Now right in front was a lazy waterwheel.
Round and round it goes as if it loves doing this.

It comes to the end of its journey.
But more drama is still to come.
Someone fell in and luckily he was saved.
Just a couple more metres to go then,
The river slothfully entered the sea.

*Trevor Earl  (12)*
*Borden Grammar School*

## DRUGS

'Sad and depressed,
Need cheering up,
Go and try one,
Have it on me.
This one's for free,
It will make you feel happy,
Take it from me!'
'I'm not sure I want to.'
'It will do no harm,'
'Thanks but no thanks,
Maybe next time,
I have enough problems without an addiction,
To a killing drug.'

*Craig Hewitt  (15)*
*Borden Grammar School*


## BASKETBALL

Basketball is my favourite sport,
Played upon a rather large court.
With slam dunks from all around,
And large feet trample the ground.
My favourite player is Michael Jordan
'Mr Air' as everyone calls him.
With Denis Rodman at Point Guard,
He's the NBA's Mr Hard.
Scottie Pippen is also brill,
Going round players with loads of skill.
Off goes the buzzer, end of the game,
And for the players immediate fame
With awards coming left, right and centre,
The players get better and better.

*Marc Powell  (15)*
*Borden Grammar School*

## EUROPE STREET

A trio of men named Mike, Chris and Pete,
were renting a flat down Europe Street.
The rent was high, a ridiculous price,
the landlord claimed he had no choice.
Another man came and spoke to the tenants,
'If he was landlord he would lower the rent.'
He claimed *Ginger* Mike was the cause of the rent,
he would get rid of Ginger and have perfect tenants.
The tenants were desperate, the rent was so high,
they willingly believed his discriminating lies.
Before long the new man ran the house,
after twenty years there, Mike was thrown out.

New owner, Mr Berlin, made good his promise,
at first the high rents were all abolished.
He seemed so good, they accepted his plan,
he would make the street perfect, he would start to expand.
At first he went next door, took Mr Pole's house,
the other landlords objected to his taking it with force.
But he went on West, taking Mr Brussels' property,
everyone saw he had not acted properly,
He had taken it with force without negotiation,
the other landlords had to act, there was no more debating.
Mr French, Mr English, Mr Red in the east,
knew now they had to tame the power of this beast.

Mr French's house was next on Berlin's list,
French received the help of the English to resist.
But soon Berlin had pushed Mr French out,
Mr French had to stay in Mr English's house.
Mr English was a problem, he was further down the street,
he may be harder for Berlin to beat,
Then Berlin made a mistake, he took a stupid risk,
he added Mr Washington to his list.
But Washington and English were just too strong,
he soon knew his choice had been very wrong.
Before long Berlin was wiped off the board,
Mr English and Mr Washington had the landlords restored.

***Charles Parkinson (15)***
***Borden Grammar School***


## THE MIGHTY SEA

Among the angry mighty sea
Huge *roaring, crashing* waves
Smash against the over-worn rocks.
The gushing sea is like 'Dragon's Power!'
Sending his might over the storm.
Lightning flashes as bright as before
God in Heaven is angry
And shaking with *'rage'!*
The weather is like a million knights
Charging at you at once.
The sea is as black as soot
in a chimney.
The waves are as *'huge'!*
as skyscrapers in Tokyo.
Suddenly the great mighty sea
fades away and all is still.

***Ben Blake (12)***
***Borden Grammar School***

## THE MOON

Under the dazzling moon
A silver mouse darts across the moonlit grass.
The moon which seems to be everlasting to the mouse
follows him in his desperate attempt to conceal himself.
All people
Great and small,
Fat and thin,
Old and young,
Lay asleep in their houses.
The orangey-brown fox shows his sparkling white
teeth ready to catch his prey.
He is ready for his chance when the mouse is unaware.
The water from which the mouse came,
The water,
So still,
Glistening is the moon,
So peaceful.

*Gregory Brissenden  (11)*
*Borden Grammar School*

## AUTUMN DAYS

Autumn days have sharp cool winds,
In the morning dead leaves are glistening
with dew on the ground.
Trees pointing their twiggy arms
in all directions.
Yellow, red, orange and brown leaves
covering the ground like multicoloured snow.

Horse chestnuts hanging loosely on the trees
waiting for children to knock them down.

Children excitedly gathering the
glossy brown conkers.

Evenings are growing longer.

A mist is lingering like a hungry cat.

*Stephen Head  (11)*
*Borden Grammar School*


# THE JUNGLE

In the jungle a herd of elephants stomp by,
Sending dust up into the sky.
A crocodile slides into a swamp,
His razor sharp teeth are to go chomp.
A giraffe eats leaves from the tallest tree,
While a parakeet flies through his knees.
A parrot squawks, it's very loud.
The sky is empty of any cloud.
A jaguar sprints after an antelope,
Whose getting away isn't much hope.
A rhino snuffles about on the ground,
His body is brown, hairy and round.
A small fish darts up the murky stream,
But his only worry is if another fish
                wants to eat him for its tea.

*Mark Foster  (11)*
*Borden Grammar School*

## WHAT SHALL I BE?

What shall I be?
An astronaut, a footballer, a rock 'n roll star?
Too unrealistic, too optimistic by far.
A librarian, a businessman, a bank manager?
No, I don't want to be old and grey,
Carrying my life in my suitcase every day,
I want to get out and live, anyway!
A policeman, an MI5 agent, a security guard?
No, I'd have to live my life by the book,
I don't want to be like a fish on a hook,
And just stand around all day with that dull, dreary look.
A writer, an actor, a Hollywood legend?
Or a thousand other ways that I have not mentioned
To be famous for ever. No that isn't me.
That's not the life for little old me.
If I'm honest, I don't have a clue what I'll be,
But I know that when I look back, when I'm old and my days are done,
I'll be able to say, 'Wasn't life fun?'

*Antony Senner (15)*
*Borden Grammar School*

# I WAS JUST

I was just seeing
  if my dog could swim,
    when suddenly the bathroom
      was flooded,

I was just trying Dad's
  razor when my dog
    suddenly had a
      bald patch,

I was just seeing if
  my dog could fly,
    when suddenly there was
      a hole in the shed roof,

I was just seeing
  if my dog had
    more than one life,

I was just seeing
  what the worst feeling
    in the world was,
        *now I know!*

***Richard Knell  (11)***
***Borden Grammar School***

## UNAIDED

I know I do not want it,
But I've got to.
Whilst I wonder why it's me,
People laugh and they smirk.

I know I do not want it,
But I've got to.
They say it helps . . . does it?
Everyone knows I'm the one . . .
With it.

I know I do not want it,
But I've got to.
It's like a nurse who sits there,
She won't go away.

I know I do not want it,
But I've got to.
What have they done to me?
Made my life hell.

I know I do not want it,
But I've got to.
What have I done to deserve . . .
*a hearing aid!*

**David Chick (11)**
**Borden Grammar School**

## ALL I WANT IS A FRIEND

There he stands solemnly,
In his field, lonely.
No one goes near,
Their hearts full of fear,
He is the *bull!*

Dreaming of company,
He stands all day,
You can see he is sad,
Everyone thinks he's bad,
He is the *bull!*

He leans on the gates,
He waits and waits,
He lets out sad cries,
Loneliness in his eyes,
He is the *bull!*

But one day,
The farmer led him away,
To a pasture with lots of cows,
Where he could play
Now he is glad,
Some new friends he has,
He is the happy *bull!*

*Martin Baker (11)*
*Borden Grammar School*

# THE FATE OF ROMEO AND JULIET

Romeo and Juliet,
Quite a couple
They're star crossed lovers
Bound to end in trouble.

They met one eve
And on the night,
It was plain to see
It was love at first sight.

Despite all the efforts
From the friar and the nurse,
It seems to me
They were under a curse.

The loved each other so
And went to be wed
In Friar Laurence's cell,
Just as the nurse said.

The couple were happy
Till Romeo was banished
For avenging the death
Of his friend so cherished.

They will meet again
But in the crypt
Where they'll stay together
For ever in sleep.

Their deaths unite
But it's too late,
Because the story ended in
*Fate!*

*Matthew Barraclough (16)*
*Borden Grammar School*

## THE COUNTRYSIDE

Rivers of concrete flow over the surface.
Cars roll along the river bed.
Eroding the land,
With pillows of black smoke,
Erupting, covering the countryside,
With a thick film of dew.

Forests of houses, tall, stationary,
Towering over their surroundings,
Offer shelter to the ants,
That scurry busily beneath them.
While wind and rain erode them,
leaving piles of rubble,
Rotting on the forest floor.

The ants scurry,
In and out of the trees,
Completing their tasks,
Crowding the concrete floor;
Some drop what they carry,
Littering the way.
Ants hurrying about their lives.

Criminals and politicians,
Prey on the unwary ants,
Ending their lives,
By taking everything away.
The predators conquer their prey,
But the predators need the ants to survive,
So they tell them some lies.

*Darren William Jones (15)*
*Borden Grammar School*

# LIFE

Life,
Like a never ending river,
Winding its long course
Over harsh rocks and smooth sand,
With all of its twists and turns.

Life,
Full of joy and rapture,
Love, passion, desire and life.
The ecstasy of living: to breathe,
To do, to be, to have, and to hold.

Life,
The harvesting of what is good,
Abandonment of what is bad,
Resisting the temptation of the dark forces,
And striving to do our level best.

Life,
The darkness after the light,
The untold pleasure, yet to behold.
Preservation, procreation
Life goes on, it always will.

Life,
the game that everyone plays,
Roll the dice, take your turn,
Make your move, find your place,
Who will win? Who will achieve the most?

Life,
Like a circle, a complete rotation,
It has no beginning, no end.
It is ever living, never forgiving,
Life will go on.

*Matthew Frayne (16)*
*Borden Grammar School*

## AWAY

Do you remember those times
When everything's wrong
When every day is a disaster zone?
It is during those days when all you need
Is to go away.

Away is a place where loved ones go
When they are needed most.
They leave you stranded,
Unintentionally misguided.
But still they're not here,
They are away.

When they're away, mistakes are made
Problems are left unresolved.
You're left feeling bad, but nothing is done
Because people are away.

*Dean Zweck (15)*
*Borden Grammar School*

## SPELLBOUND

Spellbound about the state of the environment,
Spellbound by the way that people treat one another,
Spellbound at the police in the way they react to our calls for help,
Spellbound by the ozone layer,
Spellbound by the amount of violence and mortality around,
Spellbound by the amount of hunger and starvation everywhere,
Spellbound by the *world*.

*Samantha Keeble (12)*
*Chatham Grammar School For Girls*

## SPELLBOUND BY NIGHT

Spellbound by sky, dazzling everywhere.
As your eyes start to close the stars begin to fade.
The curtains close so your dreams then open.

Spellbound by the moon looking through your window.
Staring, twinkling, turning and blinking.
Changing shape each night and day.

In the morning the sun starts to rise,
Up it comes to your eyes.
Then at night it goes again.
And in the morning it is there once again.

*Stacey Pearson (11)*
*Chatham Grammar School For Girls*


## SPELLBOUND!

The clouds rumble and crash,
The rain pelts down,
The wind whistles through the trees,
The thunder frightens children,
The lightning flashes on and off,
Like a light.

The people use umbrellas,
They are blowing to and fro,
The office workers scuttle home,
In the pouring rain.
The sun comes up,
The sky looks washed clean,
I am spellbound by the change.

*Esterina Fiore (12)*
*Chatham Grammar School For Girls*

# HAIKU

Leaves are falling, falling
As the wind is calling, calling
For autumn is finally here

*Donna Hayward (12)*
*Chatham Grammar School For Girls*


# AN AUTUMN POEM

As I lay on the ground!
The leaves fall around
On the soft ground there below.

*Laura Taylor (12)*
*Chatham Grammar School For Girls*


# SPELLBOUND

Like an enchanted fairytale land,
The waterfall gushes,
The fairies fly,
In the distance, a unicorn
On perfect pasture,
All colours glisten in a spectrum of light,
But all is not well in the mystical world,
Witches are brewing their curse of evil
Across this perfect land,
This world is most definitely,
*Spellbound.*

*Danielle Devereux (12)*
*Chatham Grammar School For Girls*

## SPELLBOUND BY CRUELTY TO DOGS

On it walks through the park
Being pulled back by its master.
The lead strangles its neck.
A cry of alarm fills the air
The master looks down,
Hitting its stomach,
Another cry.
Suddenly being kicked,
The animal keeps quiet,
Not wanting to be hurt again.
The cold air makes it shiver,
It stops, wanting breath.
The lead is taken off,
Its master is fed up.
The animal is picked up
And thrown in the road.
The master walks off,
The puppy is alone.

*Angela Hammond  (13)*
*Chatham Grammar School For Girls*


## SPELLBOUND

It wanders here and there
Scattering raindrops everywhere
It looks so bright and so fair
Floating across the sky without a care.

The cloud sails through the sky
Look at it! It's up so high!
The cloud passes by the sun
Which is beaming down on everyone.

The cloud passes through many places
Seeing so many different faces
But then the cloud will go away
To a place where he'd rather stay.

*Leyna Mendham  (13)*
*Chatham Grammar School For Girls*

## EXPOSED

Like a picture in a gallery,
They all came to see,
They looked and stared,
All eyes on me.
Undressing me with their eyes,
I hung my head low,
They poked and prodded,
Then they looked into my soul.
They laughed at my thoughts,
And cried for joy,
As I opened up my heart,
They thought my feelings were a toy.
I looked away embarrassed,
There was nothing I could say,
That was the only talent I had,
And they all refused to stay.
My soul was empty,
The gallery was now closed,
That was a part of me no one was supposed to see,
A part of me I can't believe I dared to show.

*Anisha Paddam  (13)*
*Chatham Grammar School For Girls*

## SPELLBOUND

Innocent lives,
Are taken away,
In a war of stupidity,
No one has a say.

Shocking news,
Comes every day,
The Third World really is,
In an awful way.

Those poor, poor people,
They'd rather die,
Than live like they are,
In agony they lie.

Some people don't care,
Others try to help,
But nothing's worse,
Than being there yourself.

But ask yourself,
Why do they kill?
Don't they have a conscience?
Or do they like lives to steal?

At the end of the day,
What do they achieve?
I say nothing,
Just people to cry and grieve.
I'm just spellbound.

*Shelley King (12)*
*Chatham Grammar School For Girls*

# SPELLBOUND BY THE RESTLESS SEA

A restful breeze calmly drifts across the bay,
Sweeping up sand,
And forming little waves to lap against the shore,
Crabs scuttle, dodging in and out of the ebbing tide,
And daringly, little fish swim frantically into the weeded shadows.

Slowly the sky starts to turn grey,
Then a dark black blanket covers the sky,
Engulfing the sea and its surroundings,
The wind then picks up speed,
Churning what was a beautiful blue sea,
And drowning the thoughts of that tranquil scene.

It towers high creating a devious wild cat,
With a will to devour all in its way,
Silently, it waits for the right time to pounce on its prey,
Then it lunges up pounding into the rocks,
But still it majestically drops,
The cold spray skims through the air.

Then once again it leaps at rocks and cliffs,
Scrambling up the side,
But like a helpless kitten it slips down,
Back into the depths of the ocean,
Sluggishly it sinks back down with guilt,
Leaving the sea serene and peaceful.

So once again the sun comes out,
To join the crabs and their playful humour,
But lurking down there it hides,
Waiting for its revenge.

*Lisa Bedelle  (13)*
*Chatham Grammar School For Girls*

## SPELLBOUND BY THE HOMELESS

Homeless left outside in the cold,
Left outside in a shop doorway,
A dirty, dusty, disease carrying doorway,
Homeless forgotten and not cared about,
Left to die and catch diseases,
No one caring, no one knowing how much they suffer,
Clothes hanging on by just one thread, soon they will be bare.
Clutching one another to keep from getting cold,
Children running, barely running, round and round the streets,
No homes, no gardens, no fun, no laughter, no food, no happy life,
Hundreds dying every year from starvation, cold and thirst.

*Beckie Ferguson (12)*
*Chatham Grammar School For Girls*


## SPELLBOUND BY THE WORLD

The world is being covered with a thick black cover
People are dying because there is so much pollution in the air
The world is being suffocated by you and me
People are using cars and public transport more and more
The world is dying bit by bit every day
Heat is rising and rivers are drying out
This means that more animals are dying and more starvation is
occurring
Trees are turning brown with acid rain
Seas and oceans are full of nuclear waste, the fish are poisoned and
uneatable
Dead birds lie on the beaches covered in oil
Seasons are changing and crops won't grow
People need more and more help
They are saying 'God save us all!'

*Samantha James (12)*
*Chatham Grammar School For Girls*

## SPELLBOUND

I can't believe the work of man,
I don't expect you to understand.

They cut down trees,
Not feeling guilty.

To ruin the homes of animals,
Who have nowhere to go.

Should we just turn the other way,
Not worry about what's happening today?

I can't believe the work by man,
I don't expect you to understand.

*Stacey Bell  (12)*
*Chatham Grammar School For Girls*


## CHRISTMAS TREE

C olourful lights
H andsome branches
R ed sparkle
I mages of beauty
S hiny balls of reflections
T all and slender
M any decorations to show
A ll very beautiful and bright
S ilent, but centre of attention

T winkling and sparkling
R otating and spinning
E very branch brightly
E manating warm light.

*Pamela Coothen  (12)*
*Chatham Grammar School For Girls*

## POVERTY AND WAR

The distant shriek of a gun shot,
Still ringing in the ear,
Famine, hunger and fear show in the face of every child.
Blood spills across the country,
Everyone is mourning for the life of a friend,
Families are separated during the confusion of war,

People try to run but there is nowhere to go.
A baby cries but there is nobody who can hear over the shot of a gun,
Houses are no longer homes just shelters from the wind,
As the hope of the people slowly fades,
The birds no longer sing.

The sun cannot be seen through the destruction of the war,
Even on the hottest days the country is cold,
The rivers are no longer blue but red with the blood that's been shed,
The sun lowers but will not rise until the war comes to an end.

*Lisa Woollett  (13)*
*Chatham Grammar School For Girls*


## SPELLBOUND

S pellbound by people,
P eople have ears to hear,
E yes to see and,
L ove to share,
L ove is everywhere.
B eing spellbound is what
O ur family's about,
U nder the stars you think about
N ew life, but that is only
D reaming.

*Charlotte Jessup  (11)*
*Chatham Grammar School For Girls*

## SPELLBOUND

I am spellbound by . . .
The sight of a first blossom on a tree
A red red rose, soft and shiny
The first bite of an apple crisp and fresh

I am spellbound by . . .
The first giggle of a cherub
My favourite teddy sitting waiting for me
A breath of air from Spartz

I am spellbound by . . .
A golden ray of sunshine falling down
A kitten playing with a ball
The first sight of a mother with her newborn

I am spellbound with . . .
Glass made from the cleanest sand
Gold from under the sea
Pearl sent from the Lord of all
Silver embroidered with leaves and roses

I will be spellbound when I travel . . .
To a land far away
And be washed in to a shining gate
To a place where mortals never may grace

*Hayley Usmar (12)*
*Chatham Grammar School For Girls*

# SPELLBOUND BY A MYTH

A silver shadow wanders through
The freezing snow of icy blue,
Upon its head a long gold horn,
He is the mythical *unicorn.*

He binds the ancient gods of Earth,
Upon his head is a bridle of myrrh,
Below his withers is a saddle
Of frankincense enlaced with emeralds.

He lifts his head for he has heard
A sound travelling on the wind,
He tries to conceal himself in the snow,
But no! his glistening coat's in view.

Three horses gallop onto the scene,
A streak of gold, a hint of green,
An arrow whistles past his ear,
And like a horse in frightened frenzy, he gallops far from there.

Arrows fly from side to side,
But they do not bring him down.
He gallops through a darkened wood,
Where vines and branches creep around.

His golden horn becomes entangled.
His struggles will not free him.
The men approach with daggers raised,
The gods prepare to leave us

*Charlotte Hicks  (11)*
*Chatham Grammar School For Girls*

# SPELLBOUND

Spellbound,
Theme parks,
Really fast rides,
Round and upside down
Speeding down the water flume -
Riveted!

Spellbound,
Night sky,
The comet Hale-Bopp
Flying through the galaxy,
Bright, alight, your tail aglow -
Entranced!

Spellbound,
The theatre,
Actors and actresses
Performing their mystical play,
Facing the music and dancing -
Captivated!

Spellbound,
By storms,
Lightning streaking down
Thunder crashing all around,
In the darkness of night -
Bewitched!

*Nicola Mayes  (12)*
*Chatham Grammar School For Girls*

## SPELLBOUND

Farther and farther out it flows,
Never starting, never ending.
The repeating bob going up, going down,
Gleaming in the sun like sparkling diamonds.
Turquoise blue and soapy white foam,
Joining together to make it last.
Splashing catfish and sharks' fins,
Gushing waves, everlasting dreams.
The sun's on the horizon,
The water is calm and peaceful.
Never forget the amazing sight you see,
But you can only see it,
If you are looking at the *sea!*

*Katherine Read (11)*
*Chatham Grammar School For Girls*


## SPELLBOUND

Can you imagine not having chairs,
On a cold and nasty night,
No one to put their arms around you,
No one to sit there and hold you tight,
Chairs are such wonderful things,
Very soft and comfy,
Sit down and try some one day,
Beware they might be lumpy,
Chairs are so important,
But some people don't have them,
So when you go to sit on them.
Think of those without them.

*Sarah Ayling (11)*
*Chatham Grammar School For Girls*

## WHAT IS GREEN

Green is swaying leaves,
Upon a summer's day,
But in the autumn they die,
And disintegrate into the ground.
Green is the colour of
The world of make believe.
Crunchy green grass,
On a cold winter's day.
Green is Christmas trees, holly,
And shiny ribbons too.
It is full green buses,
And the rage of people,
Who can't get on.
Munching green apples from the trees.
And wellington boots all splashed in mud,
Of ten green bottles standing on,
The wall and children singing,
Green is especially the colour,
Of the eyes of the,
One I love,
My Tigger.

*Jenna Oliver  (11)*
*Chatham Grammar School For Girls*

## SPELLBOUND

Spellbound by unnecessary killing and
Torture in the world.

I'm spellbound about the fact that
Thousands of people were killed in World War Two
Just because they were Jews.

I'm spellbound by people being murdered
Just because they were in the wrong
Place at the wrong time.

I'm spellbound by all the starvation
And poverty in the world.

I'm spellbound by all the innocent people
Who are killed because their countries are at war.

I'm spellbound by all the people who are killed and
Injured by dangerous land mines.

*Kelly Horan  (12)*
*Chatham Grammar School For Girls*

## SPELLBOUND BY REMAINS OF A WAR

Sunlight glinting on the raindrops,
Patterns thrown across the room,
Paper strewn on the table,
Shattered mirrors on the ground.

What about the morning bird call?
Who is there to hear its song?
Everything is caught for all time,
In this desolate land of hell.

Bombshells scattered all around,
Long past memories of proud people,
Lost for ever;
Gone for all time.

What about the morning bird call?
What about the past?
What about the long-gone memories
Gone for ever,
In a *blast?*

*Amy Adams (12)*
*Chatham Grammar School For Girls*


## THE MAGIC OF HALLOWEEN

A magical night,
Filled with tales of mystery,
Tales of creatures,
We never dare to imagine,
Aliens, goblins, wolves and witches,
Each year brings a new tale,
Told by friend to friend,
Now told to the creatures of the night.
As the clock strikes twelve we wonder,
Whether an extra hour has been added.
An hour when it is no longer our party,
And the children will again run across the roads,
Screaming trick or treat.
Some costumes can look so real,
That the witches may be witches,
And the goblins may be goblins.
And I find myself spellbound by the magic of Halloween.

*Carla O'Hagan (12)*
*Chatham Grammar School For Girls*

## THE WORLD OF THE FAMOUS

The world of the famous how fortunate they are,
Surrounded by great expensive cameras,
Flashing bright sparkles in their eyes,
They're always the centre of attention,
Fashion designers, to transform their complexion,
Homes the size of a palace,
With their currency they can afford anything,
All their wishes are granted,
To be live on the big, square screen,
Always fan-mail knocking down their doors,
Outfits that cost a year's allowance,
Going on voyages to countries around the globe,
Attractive faces that people admire,
Their whole life is our dream.

*Paula Cross  (11)*
*Chatham Grammar School For Girls*


## ALL ALONE

The world is so empty,
As I look around,
There is no one else,
Only me.

When you isolate,
This from something else,
You will soon see,
The world is so deserted.

I'm the only one,
Who can see,
That this empty world,
Could be such fun.

*Vicki Smith  (12)*
*Chatham Grammar School For Girls*


## THE TIGER

I hear a roar,
Then I see a black and white paw,
A smiling face,
A lick of the lips,
And a glint of a shining tooth.

His black and beady eyes follow my every move,
He digs at the ground with his long claws,
He moves closer,
I gasp,
I freeze.

He sniffs at me,
Then licks my arm,
I stare in terror,
He opens his mouth,
I see a long row of sharp teeth.

Then there is a rustle,
A little sniff,
Then the tiger,
Gracefully,
Runs away.

*Angela Duffett  (11)*
*Chatham Grammar School For Girls*

# MAGIC

It's a weird, wonderful
object in life it's mysterious
and can be dangerous
but with a magical
thrill.
Used by witch and human,
cauldrons with bubbles
and steam with a
significant smell of
substances which can only
be described by an
abnormal force for a
bounce of energy.

A lift in life, a stifling
strength as a superstitious
feeling comes across
for a reason to throw
the dice and see what
happens.
Magic is there if you
want it.

*Katie-Jayne Alston  (11)*
*Chatham Grammar School For Girls*

## NATURE

We are surrounded by it,
Although we can't always see it,
It is beautiful,
But we destroy it,
Wonderful it may be,
Humans just can't see,
That we need to stop destruction,
To enable it to grow,
It is nature,
All creatures big and small,
Need it all,
For all different reasons,
All through the seasons,
The cats need it to hunt,
So their claws don't become blunt,
Birds need it to hide,
After their long ride,
Insects need it to lay their eggs,
So we need to get thinking,
Or the world will be stinking,
Of dead trees and smoke,
Take care of what we have,
Because if we destroy it today,
It won't be there tomorrow.

*Charlotte Pattenden  (11)*
*Chatham Grammar School For Girls*

## THE DESTRUCTION OF NATURE

Spellbound by the spirit and gracefulness of nature
I wonder how animals manage to survive the damages
mankind has inflicted,
Disease, poverty and pollution destroys both people
and animals.
The great hunt for skins and pelts of big cats, wolves,
bears and gorillas still goes on.
Even though humans have noticed these mighty creatures,
still the hunt goes on.
Not just land creatures are in danger, marine life as well.
Shark fins are used for Chinese medicine,
Whales are used too.

How will the creatures of this
savage world ever survive?

*Suzanne Pert  (11)*
*Chatham Grammar School For Girls*

## BABIES

Why?
Why do their little hearts beat?
Why do people help them?
Do they really care?

Do they know
What it's like?
Maybe they do.
Or maybe not.

Small babies crying,
People helping,
Do the babies know,
How people are helping?

*Sarah Hodge  (12)*
*Chatham Grammar School For Girls*


## SPELLBOUND BY DAWN

I looked out of the window,
Mist curled round the tree,
Like a kitten chasing its tail,
A spider's web on the fence,
Like a fisherman's net catches the mist,
And turns it into diamonds, glinting in the sun.
A flock of starlings settle on the lawn,
Pecking hungrily at the crumbs.
Dew from an overhanging tree,
Drops into the cool silver pond,
As a golden fish surfaces for a moment,
And then dives down into the cool depth.
I open my window,
Spellbound by dawn,
And breathe in the new day.

*Niamh Mahon  (11)*
*Chatham Grammar School For Girls*

## SPELLBOUND BY THE BULLY

Picking on me,
Poking me,
Calling me names,
Frighten, scared,
Worrying all night. What will happen
in the playground?
Next day arrive at school - they're over there,
I'll hide. Have they seen me?
Oh, what shall I do?
They're coming over run, run I can't,
I'm caught. Help!
I scream, I shout.
They have written something on the wall.
Watch this space?

*Rebecca Metcalf (11)*
*Chatham Grammar School For Girls*

## SPELLBOUND

Hallowe'en is the night,
When ghostly ghosts appear,
When witches assemble their broomsticks,
And black cats with green eyes
Bring you good luck.

Children go trick-or-treating
And dress up as witches,
Goblins, red devils and ghosts.
At twelve o'clock, midnight,
They all disappear until 31st October
*Next year.*

*Danielle Sussex  (11)*
*Chatham Grammar School For Girls*

## SPELLBOUND

I'm spellbound by people,

How we speak,
How everyone is different,
How every person is special in one's own way,

I'm spellbound by people,

The way we laugh and smile,
The way we understand each other,
The way we help one another,

I'm spellbound by people,

How we cope with every tragedy that comes,
How we never stop believing,
How we always carry on.

*Adelle Walsh  (11)*
*Chatham Grammar School For Girls*

## SPELLBOUND

Fixing my eyes
Rooted to the spot
Becoming absorbed
No sensations outside my vision
Pleasure, fear
Focused
Warmth
Tingling, pins and needles
Flight
Fight
Calmness
Acceptance, need
Disturbance
Distraction
Movement
Disentangled, disengaged
Detachment
Rejection
Separation
End.

*Alice Johnson  (11)*
*Chatham Grammar School For Girls*

## A BED

A bed,
A body rester,
A dream maker,
An untirer,
A flop-on-dozer,
A comfortable snoozer,
A recover,
A teddy bear rester,
A late for maker,
A lazy dog helper,
A warm and *crazy* sleeper,
An automatic dozer,
A sleepy retirer,
A soft and floppy relaxer,
A body warmer,
A night-time keep safe,
A drifty dreamer,
A morning too soon,
A dumping ground,
A sleepy paradise,
And just an evening comfort!

*Kailey Guest  (11)*
*Chatham Grammar School For Girls*

## SPELLBOUND BY AUTUMN

An enchanted world,
Of rich vibrant colours,
Little animals forage,
To survive the passionless winter,
An orange carpet on the street,
The crispy leaves crunch,
When a thousand children rush over them,
Making the ground dust,
Conkers are being collected,
And demolished.

Our noses are bright red,
And we have blue, iced feet,
The winds blow silently,
But are stronger each day,
Woolly coats are appearing,
And Jack Frost is helping,
To make pretty pictures,
Days are drawing in,
Nights are expanding,
That is why autumn is spellbound.

*Joanne Ware  (11)*
*Chatham Grammar School For Girls*

## SPELLBOUND - LOVE

Love beautiful and bright but not understood,
We want to be loved but can we love?
Friends and family all around,
I'm spellbound by the way they love,
I am sure I love them back,
Do they feel the same way?
Spellbound by the hug of my mum,
The voice of a friend,
The kiss of a boy,
A shiver down my spine,
Do I love?
Can I love?
Yes, I love my family,
But do I love him?
Love, not understood,
Can anyone understand love?
Does anyone love as much as they want to be loved?
Can anyone love as much as they want to be loved?
Friends love,
Family love,
So do I,
Love is a funny thing.

*Kerry Prescott  (11)*
*Chatham Grammar School For Girls*

## SPELLBOUND

A child chased a dog away
And a vixen chased her prey
She plots away at her pursuit
Her plans are always most acute
She'll use her overpowering will
And then she'll go in for the kill
She'll then select her next meal
And all that her prey will feel
Will be the fierce grip of teeth
And her tongue gripping underneath
After this the horseman came
And started with their bloody game
Then they let the hounds away
Which chased the fox day after day
The fearsome noise of the horn
The fox had heard since she was born
And now that they have caught her
The fox's name is down for slaughter.

*Elizabeth Hazell (11)*
*Chatham Grammar School For Girls*

## SPELLBOUND BY THE FOUR SEASONS

Snowflakes drifting down,
Like cotton wool flying through the air.
Swirling around you,
Freezing cold.
Nobody knows when it's going to go.

A flower grows, and leaves appear,
This is a lovely time of the year.
Animals awake from their hibernation,
Colour is everywhere.
Spring is ending.

Summer is here,
The hottest time of the year.
The sun is shining,
In the sky.
Children running around.

The leaves begin to fall from trees,
And crumble as you walk on them.
Yellow, orange, brown and green,
Winter is here again.

*Claire McGilloway (11)*
*Chatham Grammar School For Girls*

## SPELLBOUND

The stars glitter,
High above our head
Sometimes you feel
you could fly,
to touch their
shiny surface.

The moon with the
stars,
Shines so bright,
Casting its ghostly,
glow across the world,
Shimmering with the clouds.

The planets are dotted
across the night
sky,
Some have haloes,
making them angelic,
Others just look beautiful.

Space is what
keeps me spellbound,
Mysterious and silent,
Things are there
then they are gone,
That's what keeps me

*Spellbound!*

*Natalie Phillips  (12)*
*Chatham Grammar School For Girls*

## THE WAY I FEEL

My mood was as dark as night.
As my mind is full of fright.
As the bully haunts me day and night.
He makes me feel like a raging volcano,
vicious and aggressive.
My life is falling apart as I have not got the
heart to confess what's happening to me.
I never thought it would ever happen to me.

*Stuart Fallows  (12)*
*Dartford West Boy's School*

## MY FRIEND ALIEN

I was in bed when
I heard a whizz!
I looked, I saw nothing
The next night a light
lit the sky all colours,
shining brightly in
the sky.

Suddenly a light lit up
the room.
The light was coming
closer to me.
I was in fright.

It looked white and mean
big black eyes, smelling,
big head, keen and hungry,
he stopped and stared at
me he reached out, he touched
me he felt cold.

All of a sudden he
zapped away - disappeared
into the bright night.

*Adam Archer  (12)*
*Dartford West Boy's School*

# LONELINESS

No one to talk.
No one to understand.
All you can do is walk.
Walk to another land.

You're feeling, oh so sad,
people despise you.
You get treated like you did
something bad.
People say you belong in a zoo.

Nobody you can love.
Nobody cares.
When you look above
you get horrible sneers.

I know how you feel,
don't run away.
You know it's real,
everything's gonna be okay.

*Jamie Fairman  (14)*
*Dartford West Boy's School*

# IT

It came up to me,
It got me,
But it did not hurt me,
It just teased me,
And then it squeezed me,
I stopped breathing,
I got in a panic,
And then it let go,
I screamed for help,
It was no good,
I was stuck there,
Then a great beam came down,
It took me up,
Up I went,
I closed my eyes,
And then,
And then,
I woke up in my bed,
I was sweating like a pig,
My mum came in,
'What have you been doing Tim?'

*Luke Johnson (12)*
*Dartford West Boy's School*

## TEACHERS

I hate teachers and teachers hate me.
You think they can't see me talking over there.
Then she spots me, I think she must have a
radio transmitter in her hair.

The worst ones are the PE teachers.
They see you doing something wrong.
They shout and everyone will flee except me.
I will get told off and stung like a bee,
everyone watching me.
They tell you off and shout and shout and scream
Their bad breath hits you like a laser beam.

I hate teachers and teachers hate me.

*Tony Allen  (12)*
*Dartford West Boy's School*

## JASMINE (MY LITTLE SISTER)

My little sister's only 10 months,
But you should see what she can munch,
Almost anything you see,
She even tries to eat me!

Dead flies if not picked up,
She even tries the faggy buts,
Bits of paper and her shoe,
We just don't know what to do.

*You should see what's in her nappy.*
*When cleared up, all is*
*Happy!*

*Alisha Birch  (11)*
*Hartsdown Technology College*

## THE FINAL CURTAIN

It's all over now,
The final curtain crashing down on my love
With a heart of solid steel,
I pick up the pieces of my broken mind,
No more sweet caresses,
With only myself for company.
No one's to be trusted,
They'd soon drop you like a stone,
Bitterness helps you realise
You don't need anyone anyway,
The funny thing is,
Love's turned to sheer hate,
I no longer yearn for his comforting warmth,
I don't want to know him,
It's all over now.

*Anita Twells  (15)*
*Hartsdown Technology College*


## VICTORY

*V* ast amounts of people cheer and clap with joy,
*I* nside the place erupts, flags wave, people sing,
*C* ould this be the one moment of pride for the people,
*T* eddy squares after work from Gazza, Shearer scores!
*O* h what a goal for the people! A united kingdom,
*R* oaring England finish the Dutch,
*Y* ou'll never walk alone and for a time England is as one.

*Amir Eshaghzadeh  (15)*
*Hartsdown Technology College*

# WAR

War causes hatred,
People sad and depressed,
Gangs like to kill just for fun,
The people had families and friends.

Planes flying over our heads,
Dropping bombs on homes,
Homes of our friends and families,
Sad faces pollute the world,
Infecting us all - traumatised.

*Amy Ramshead (15)*
*Hartsdown Technology College*

# SCHOOL DINNERS

School dinners are yuck,
They taste like muck,
Pickle sandwiches are much better!
Roast lamb tastes like wood,
You'd saw it if you could!

My friend likes school dinners,
I think she's mad.
School dinners are foul,
They taste really bad!

Sticky semolina, over sell-by jam,
Mouldy roast potatoes and soft squidgy ham,
These are the horrors of school dinners,
People who eat sandwiches are winners!

*Louise Caudrey (13)*
*Hartsdown Technology College*

# DIGBY (MY DOG)

You are the one who listens when I walk,
the one who cheers my lonely walk.
You are the one who nuzzles when I cry,
the one who comforts when I sigh.

Who else could match my every mood,
who else would feast on scraps of food.
Who else would prompt this monologue,
who else but you? My loving dog, Digby.

*Danny Rouse (15)*
*Hartsdown Technology College*

# IN THE CORNER OF THE SCHOOL PLAYGROUND

I see the pain, in the corner of the school playground.
I see bullying, in the corner of the school playground.
I see three children bullying a smaller and weaker child,
in the corner of the school playground.
I see three children pushing, shoving, deciding to kick
and punch, in the corner of the school playground.
I hear obscenities shouted at a poor individual,
in the corner of the school playground.
I see the wrong colour hair, height, weight, liking the
wrong things, in the corner of the school playground.
It is not his fault, everyone is different. Admire other
people for what they are not.
Don't hate others for what they are.

*Ben Wolstenhulme (15)*
*Hartsdown Technology College*

## My Grandad

My grandad is an old man, experience of life,
My grandad is an old man, kind, generous,
always there,
My grandad is an old man, he survived the war,
My grandad is an old man still suffering from
the wound,
He will never forgive,
He will never forget.

*Tom Faulkner (15)*
*Hartsdown Technology College*


## Love?

What is love? I know not what it is.
Is love the feeling of happiness?
If so, I must be in love
But what or who with?
Is love the feeling of warmth?
Clothes keep me warm but I don't
love.
Is love forgiveness?
It can't be, I forgive who sin against me.
How do you find love?
Do you stumble against it?
Is it hiding?
Is it underneath the dark clouds of hate?
What is love?
Will I ever find out?

*Nadine Hill (15)*
*Hartsdown Technology College*

## REMEMBER

Sometime when you're feeling important
Sometime when your ego's in bloom
Sometime when you take it for granted
You're the best qualified man in the room

Sometime when you feel that your going
Would leave an unfillable hole
Just follow this simple instruction
And see how it humbles your soul

Take a bucket and fill it with water
Put your hands in it up to your wrists
Pull them out - and the hole that remains
Is a measure of how you'll be missed

You may splash all you please as you enter
You may stir up the waters galore
But stop and you'll see in a minute
It looks just the same as before

The moral of this is quite simple
Do just the best that you can
Be proud of yourself - but remember
There is no indispensable man.

*Tracie Ogles  (16)*
*Hartsdown Technology College*

## THE SEASONAL STAIN

As leaves start to fall,
and the cold winds call.

The rain grows harder,
the same temperamental Lada.

More people sneezing,
as the weather starts freezing.

The frost on the ground,
the same seasonal sound.

Then the days get short,
an atmospherical fault.

As Christmas draws near,
Christian children cheer.

The New Year comes,
and new winds hum.

The spring comes along,
the same Easter songs.

As the summer comes along,
the seas and beaches throng.

Then autumn comes again,
with the same seasonal stain.

*Matthew Still  (13)*
*Hartsdown Technology College*

## EMOTIONS

I feel like a thunderstorm
running down very fast
making rivers in my head.

I feel like the sun rising
in the sky
reflecting on the streets.

I feel like a jumping kangaroo
jumping around all day
waiting for the surprise.

I feel like the only
thing on earth that's
waiting for something
to happen.

I feel like rain rushing
down very fast
but when it stops, I feel
like the sunset has risen.

*Tara Osborn  (12)*
*Robert Napier School*

## EMOTIONS

When I'm angry I feel like
a volcano getting hot and
bothered then erupting, throwing
bucketfuls of lava everywhere.

When I'm happy I feel like a
sun shining on a Caribbean sea.

When I'm sad my eyes feel
like rain clouds just about to burst.

When I feel excited I feel like
a grass hopper, hopping.

When I'm bored, I feel like a
cardboard box in a dark attic corner.

When I'm lonely, I feel like a dog in
a kennel full of cats.

When I'm scared, I feel like a four-eyed
green blob monster is gobbling me up.

*Paul Hyland  (11)*
*Robert Napier School*

## EMOTIONS

I feel like a thunderstorm
crashing to the ground.
I feel like a bird whizzing
through the meadow.
I feel like a flower dying
in a flowerpot.
I feel like I'm drowning in
a bowl of water.
I feel as though I'm floating
around the room.
My mind is filled with different
signs telling me which way to go.

*Danielle Cockwell  (11)*
*Robert Napier School*

## EMOTIONS

When I feel angry, I feel like a thunderstorm
smashing on houses.
When I'm excited, I feel like running the biggest
marathon.
When I'm stressed, I feel like trashing the world
and turning the lights out.
When I'm happy, I feel like doing anything that
people ask me.

*Rhys Adams  (11)*
*Robert Napier School*

## EMOTIONS

When I'm angry my blood starts to boil
like a really big volcano's lava running down
the side.

When I'm sad, my tears fall down my face
like a great big waterfall.

When I'm scared, my body trembles like
an earthquake hitting San Francisco.

When I'm shocked, my eyes widen, my mouth
opens as round as a wheel going round.

When I'm nervous my teeth chatter like a
woodpecker hitting a great big tree.

*Kerri Cook  (11)*
*Robert Napier School*




## CHOCOLATE

I like chocolate, it is the best.
I like it melting in my mouth.
I sit cosy in my house.
I sit by the fireplace and have a rest.
Eating my chocolate all day long.
I just sit there all day long.

*Kelly Powell  (14)*
*Rowhill School*

## MIDNIGHT

The night is long, the moon is clear,
  As a hunter stalks a grazing deer
In and out, of the trees they dash,
  Branches removed by the hunter's thrash.

Suddenly he halts, poised for a shot,
  Sweat on his brow, sticky and hot,
He misses by inches, yet it shakes the deer,
  He's gaining every moment, closing in on her rear.

Once again the chase is on,
  Yet soon the moon, will have to be gone,
The sun awakes on the eastern side,
  Spreading her radiance far and wide.

As the early birds caw their morning cry,
  The hunter heaves a sorrowful sigh,
The deer is away, but she's had a scare,
  Happy to be free, yet still cautious and aware.

He turns around and trudges home,
  Empty-handed and alone,
Tomorrow he'll be back, using mind and skill,
  Ready and awaiting, to make his final kill.

*Amy Watt  (12)*
*St Catherine's RC School*

## WHO'S THAT?

I looked into a mirror and saw someone just
like me.
They wore my coat and my trousers, with the
patch upon the knee.
I tried to walk away but they just followed
me around.
And when I got tired, we both sat down.

I tried and tried to shake him off but I just
couldn't succeed.
Then suddenly I realised, that person was *me!*

*Anna Coughlan  (13)*
*St Catherine's RC School*


## CASTING A SHADOW

For hours I sit here in suspense,
watching the waves as they crash on each other,
like lost children looking for somewhere to go,
As seagulls glide across the sky with no worries or cares
for the rest of the world around them,
And the wind blowing with all its might, blows against my
bare face, sending chills down my spine,
And the sun setting as I sit here alone casting a shadow.

The water is calm and has brought a deafening silence,
The air is still,
My heart racing faster than before,
Darkness is near,
Seagulls have gone to their rest,
But I still sit here alone casting a shadow.

*Tracey Duodu  (11)*
*St Catherine's RC School*

## What's In A Face

Two eyes, a nose and a mouth and lips.
A changing statement of feeling.
A fleeting glimpse of life.
The sheer happiness of a war now won,
that appears on the survivors face.

The deep guilt of a secret crime.
The humiliation about to erupt into rage.
The blank stare that denies emotion.
The fierce blaze of anger tearing the
soul to shreds.
The deep sorrow that refuses comfort.
The bewilderment that comes clear when
a problem is solved.

A fearful frown.
An ugly grimace.
A beaming smile.
An arrogant air.
A weary, worried look.
A face without an expression is like a
picture without colour.

*Francesca Purbrick  (11)*
*St Catherine's RC School*

## ARMS OF GOD

As I sat there holding his hand,
Thinking of the past.
He gave me a gentle,
But sweet smile,
And that was to be his last.
I never said I loved you,
I never said goodbye,
Now in the arms of God,
No more tears can I cry,
For our love will never die.

*Samantha Butler (12)*
*St Catherine's RC School*


## AUTUMN

The leaves are starting to fall, there's a nip in the air.
It won't be long 'til the trees are all bare.

The mornings are getting darker, the lights are all on,
I notice that the corn in the fields is all gone.

From the canopy of brown conkers on the floor,
I do find picking fallen apples is a very boring chore.

Short shirts are being put away,
I think the Harvest Festival is on Sunday.

All these signs make it clear, that autumn time is
certainly here . . .

*Catherine Sandion (12)*
*St Catherine's RC School*

## ONE SMILE

Will my worries
never go away?

Yet again
I face another day.

Quietly I sit
on my own,

Sometimes I wish
someone would phone.

What does it take
to meet new people?

Then I find one
smile is what you
send,

And then it bridges
the gap between
friends.

*Debbie Laszcz  (12)*
*St Catherine's RC School*

## WHEN BETTY EATS SPAGHETTI

When Betty eats spaghetti
She slurps, she slurps, she
slurps.

When Betty eats spaghetti
she burps, she burps, she
burps.

Her mother said 'Betty
if you slurp your spaghetti
so fast, you will burp
and burp and burp.

*Emma Munro  (11)*
*St Catherine's RC School*


## FAIRIES

Down at the bottom of the garden,
with all the birds and the bees,
Lives a swarm of fairies hiding in the trees,
There is lots of magic if only you could see,
So come and join the fairy swarm and magic
all with me.
Amongst the fun and laughter there is business
being discussed,
Oh I must, oh I must know, what they are saying,
through all the fairy dust.

Now it's time for bed, I must be on my way,
I will certainly return on another day,
I know they will be waiting for me,
And when I come, greet me with glee!

*Alexandra Proctor  (12)*
*St Catherine's RC School*

## OH FLOWER OF MINE

Oh little flower, neighbour of mine
Can you teach me how to tell the time?
On a summer's day it's hard to know
As the days are long, so very very long, so
Can you teach me to tell the time
Oh little flower of mine.
The marigolds sing songs of praise
To sing I may, that one day
I will learn to tell the time
My little flower, oh flower of mine.

*Jayne Cooter  (11)*
*St Catherine's RC School*

## GRANDAD

Grandad,
His gentle touch upon my cheek
So loving, so warm
Unforgettable

His pacing stroll
A great big stride
His eyes so full of life

Now it's time to say goodbye
Up with God
In the big blue sky

He is missed oh, so very much
But never will he be gone from our
Minds and hearts.

*Laura Stoneham  (11)*
*St Catherine's RC School*

## School Sucks!

I am in my English class,
I sit and watch the minutes pass.
I cannot wait till half past three,
When the day is done
And I am free.
I still have one hour to go,
I really wish the day would flow.
The bell rings right through my ears,
The teacher said 'Goodbye my dears.'
I rush all the way to history class,
I bash the six formers as I pass.
Come 'ere they say, in a right old state,
Not now, I say or I will be late.
I take my place in the middle row,
I forgot my homework, so I will just stay low.
Guess what I'm thinking, I will give you a clue,
Only fifteen more minutes and the day is through.
        *Hooray.*

**Lauren Cooter  (13)**
**St Catherine's RC School**


## Dear Diana

Loads of people laying flowers,
People waiting hours and hours,
To see your beautiful coffin glow,
We don't want to see you go.

You really had a beautiful smile,
We just want to wait awhile,
Before we have to say goodbye,
Never see the twinkle in your eye.

You and Dodi in the sky,
Most of the rumours were a lie,
The photo men won't get away,
For some day they will have to pay.

As you passed on Friday night,
I watched as people thought, at the sight,
For heaven you've been given the key,
You're surely the Queen of Hearts to me.

*Jennifer Keogh  (11)*
*St Catherine's RC School*

# THINGS I LIKE

I like my bunny
her name is Misty
her black fur is really silky.
One of the reasons I really like her
is that she listens and understands me.

Misty has a sister called Chloe
who is my sister's bunny.
The man in the pet shop told us
that they were born on exactly
the same day.

I think her ears are really floppy
and her tail when she hops
looks really funny.
When you look into her eyes
all you can see is
a brown round circle.

*Maggie Carroll  (12)*
*St Catherine's RC School*

## I HATE SCHOOL

I've been standing here for ages as the bus is late,
I'm dreading a detention while I wait.
I finally arrive at the dreaded place,
A teacher outside, so I speed up my pace.

The books in my bag weigh a ton,
I'll be glad when this day is done.
I run along to the history class,
The work I'm given is the hardest task.

The lesson is over and break has begun,
Maths is the next awful lesson to come.
I hope I get all my algebra right,
Or another detention looms in sight.

It will soon be lunch time and I'll be free,
Then back to cross-country in PE.
Roll on last lesson in the English class,
Where I'll be happy at long, long, last.

*Kerry Collins  (12)*
*St Catherine's RC School*


## THINGS I HATE

I hate cobwebs and spiders
Rats and creepy-crawlies too
What would I do if I saw some
I'd scream and cry for you.

I hate brussel sprouts and cabbage
When my mum puts them on my plate
What do I do when I see them there
I leave them on my plate

Getting up in the morning is another hate
of mine
I'd like to stay in bed all day
And dream, George Clooney's mine.

*Lisa Wakem (12)*
*St Catherine's RC School*

## GIRLS

What are girls?

Boys think we are there to clean up after them,
Do their ironing and not to mention the washing
they leave around the place just for us to pick up
and clean.

Well I'll change that in years to come,
I will be the perfect little mum.
But acting the wife what will I do?
Plan my revenge on one or two.

But then again I could just be a sweet cute
darling little angel . . . naaaah forget it
who wants to be an angel? *Not me!*

*Amanda O'Brien (12)*
*St Catherine's RC School*

## A POEM OF IMAGINATION

As I sleep in my warm bed
videos playing in my head
veering onto a wild ride
surfing on the midnight tide

Images arrive unbid
under my quilt I'm hid
but not from own thought
in whose nightmare caught

With the dawn, all disappears
ideas, wondering, vivid fears
awaken from excited slumber
dull and dreary alarm clock thunder.

*Anne-Marie Kennedy (11)*
*St Catherine's RC School*


## THE THINGS I HATE!

I hate Diana being dead,
Lying there in her coffin of lead.

Everyone is so sad,
They're blaming the 'Press',
For being so bad.

She got her inspiration from Mother Theresa,
But now she's gone, now we have neither.

No one could beat the Queen of Hearts,
She'll always be near and will never part.

*Aideen Gormley (12) & Rebecca Sanchez (12)*
*St Catherine's RC School*

## MY FIRST DAY

Walking up the path to catch the bus.
A new uniform and it's weird.
As I await anxiously, talking to my friends.
I hear a big *grrr* . . .
Oh no, it's here,
I take my first step on to the bus.
Half an hour and I'm frightened because
We are nearly there!

We are here.
I meet my form teacher and she takes a register.
We walk and talk, me and my friends to the drama studio.
Me and my friends, nervous and scared.

We drop our bags slowly, then we go and take a seat,
I sit there wondering what to do.

The teacher's talking
The teacher's giving directions on what to do,
And oh, I'm getting confused.

Assembly's over.
We go to the form room, and oh, I'm petrified
Butterflies in my stomach.
After a while, I'm happy and new.

Everything's brand new.
Days go by and more days.
Oh I'm happy in my new school.

*Chloe Mutepha (11)*
*Swan Valley Community School*

## THE FIRST DAY

On the first day I was excited,
Opened the wardrobe,
And got out my uniform.
Pressed all neatly and tidily.
Put it on, it felt great,
All of it white and navy.
Ran downstairs, ate my breakfast,
Got my bag.
Put on my coat,
Sophie came round, we walked to the coach.
Waited for about five minutes.
Then from around the corner
It came, the coach.
We all jumped on, full of anguish.
It was good but different.
I arrived at school, nervous,
But excited
We went in, had two lessons
Went home and I couldn't wait
Until the next day.

*Samantha Higgins  (11)*
*Swan Valley Community School*


## MY NEW SCHOOL

I'm here, Swan Valley at last!
My junior school now in the past.
New uniform, new books too,
There's just so much to do.

Brand new subjects for me to do,
English, Maths and Science too,
Geography, French and PSE,
That's all too much for me.

Different teachers, some are cool,
Others are either small or tall.
Fair and dark, blonde or gold,
A few of them are big and bold.

School dinners are really great
Especially on a great big plate.
Pizzas, chips, gravy and meat,
There's just so much to eat!

*Daniel Spires  (12)*
*Swan Valley Community School*

## My New School

I'm excited going to my new school,
But nervous too.
I'm excited going to my new school.
I'm really excited to get there
But don't know what to do.
I'm getting to my new school
Feeling more petrified than ever.
I'm getting to my new school,
Thinking about the weather.
I've got to my new school
Walking down the path
I've got to get to my new school
I'm in my new school,
Sitting by my desk,
Having a rest.

*Joanne Ancill  (11)*
*Swan Valley Community School*

## MY FIRST DAY AT SWAN VALLEY

I woke up early, I was feeling bad,
I was given a lift to the bus stop by my dad.
'Don't worry,' my mum had said,
But I just kept feeling that sense of dread.
We made it to the school with teachers outside,
I just wanted to run and hide.

We all stood quietly, there's no fuss,
Perhaps there's someone stalking us.
We all walked into the drama hall,
All morning we were told what was going
To happen, what we were going to do,
But all I felt like saying was '*Tooda-loo*!'

After lunch we lined up for music,
Our first lesson today,
Music's not so bad, so, okay!
Our teacher said to write the rules
from the board,
All of a sudden I felt I was being called,
It's the clock, yes it must be,
Won't be long until half past three.

*Hollie Brown  (11)*
*Swan Valley Community School*

## HOMEWORK HORROR

I hate to do my homework,
It makes me feel so bad.
I don't do it excitedly,
Though my teachers say I should.
I hate to do my homework,
I'd love to miss a day.
I hate doing my homework,
There's more the next day.

*Adam Godfrey  (11)*
*Swan Valley Community School*

## MY NEW SCHOOL

At the bus stop I was nervous,
When the coach came I was quite happy.
The school was big,
New equipment.
Sometimes I got bored.
At the end of the day I thought it wasn't so bad.

The next day it was fun at the bus stop
I got on the coach and sat next to Kevin
We had a laugh on the way.
When we got there, we went straight to our form.
The day went quickly
When we went home I had a good day.

*Jason Saward  (11)*
*Swan Valley Community School*

# MY SCHOOL

Where we go to school
We have to follow the rules.
The classes are small
But the school is tall.

On the first day I was alarmed
On the second I was calm.
On the third I knew my way
My teachers have a lot to say.

The teachers are friendly
The children are too
We put our hands up to go to the loo.

We learn lots of new things
Then we start to sing.
Our teacher says 'Oh, what a din.'

We do English, maths and science too.
I know I'll be happy till the day is through.
Will be back tomorrow to start anew
And there're lots more things for us to do.

We do PE in the hall,
We have to throw and catch the ball.
If you drop it you are out,
All the class will scream and shout.

We wear our uniforms,
We all look smart.
My school will always be in my heart.

*Vicky Burgum  (11)*
*Swan Valley Community School*

## MY SCHOOL

Today I'm rather excited,
It's my first day back at school.
Today I'm trying really hard,
Not to break a rule.

Today it's all so quiet,
Next week there'll be a riot.
He'll say it's her and she'll say it's him,
Whatever the way, things look dim.

This week while I was eating lunch
You couldn't even hear them munch.
Next week I bet you anything
You won't be able to even think.

The teachers are all so very nice,
But if you misbehave,
They'll squash you like tiny mice
So if you're good you're safe.

It's the end of our first week at school,
Nobody's broken a rule.
Everybody's singing, what a wonderful school.

So maybe I exaggerated,
The school just isn't that bad.
And now I'm glad I started
To come here makes me glad.

*Louise Lynch  (12)*
*Swan Valley Community School*

## In Our New School

The school is fun, the school is great!
The teachers are quite friendly,
The school has new equipment,
The school is small.
The food is great.
I sometimes play football,
Other times I just walk with a friend.
There are lots of activities after school.
I have packed lunch,
I do football and badminton,
I like tennis.

*Deke Day (11)*
*Swan Valley Community School*


## School Poem

Feeling nervous and afraid,
standing there at the bus stop.
I saw a lady using a map.
I said 'Hi,' then she'd gone in a flash.
I felt scared, and I nearly fainted,
and when I awoke I was at school.
And at the end of the day I felt great
sitting on the bus with all my friends,
thinking what a lovely day I'd had
at my new school.
Getting off the bus, walking to my house,
when I arrived I told them
what a lovely day I'd had at my new school.

*Samantha Knight (11)*
*Swan Valley Community School*

## A New School

A new school,
A school of rules,
New homework,
New school,
New lessons,
New form,
New day,
New year,
And a new beginning for
Everyone.

*Katie Blake (12)*
*Swan Valley Community School*

## My First Day At School

I was nervous, scared and confused.
Everywhere I went people looked
and stared at you.
The rooms were like houses.
Some of the kids were petrified.
The work was hard and modern,
the dinners were disgusting and expensive.
The equipment was nice
and must have cost a fortune.
Teachers were friendly and then turned moany.
Then the work got confusing and muddling for me.
Then the bell went and it was time
to go home and watch TV.

*Michelle Lyons (11)*
*Swan Valley Community School*

# IN OUR NEW SCHOOL

A new school,
New rules,
New woodwork tools,
Old-fashioned teachers,
New work,
New homework.

New books,
New friends.

New pens,
New pencils,
New rulers,
New lessons,
New classes.

*Paul Ingram  (11)*
*Swan Valley Community School*


# IN OUR NEW SCHOOL

A new school but we are still getting older,
Growing up, learning different things.
New teachers, new principal.
Different school,
New subjects.
More homework.
Lots of books,
Happy school,
Happy me.

*Tom Foord  (11)*
*Swan Valley Community School*

## THE CANDLE IN THE DARKNESS

The fire burning in the darkness
Of the candle in the shadows
The light flickering in the wind
The scent of the candle sends out hope
The light is glowing brighter as the flame
Begins to melt
It's melting now, the smoke's pouring through
The heat, the warmth is slowly
Disappearing
The shape, the size is very, very little
As the candle's melting
Beneath the stars of the candle in the night
The candle's flame has disappeared
Into the darkness of the night.

*Sadie Wood (12)*
*The Abbey School*


## SEEING ANOTHER WORLD

As I see another world I see the outer limits
Shattered fragments
I see thousands of millions of the same thing
It's like a sunflower of faces
I gaze into what looks like the sun
The light reflects into loads of prisms
Or if I look ahead I see a spiral shape
Colours blend and things bend around
People morph into weird blobs
Then it changes to normal
The strange world has gone.

*Liam Richards (13)*
*The Abbey School*

## THE EYES OF A FLY

As I fly through the sky I see hundreds of things
Spirals and shapes I see
Light so bright, it is nearly blinding
The world is like a shattered bottle smashed into a hundred pieces
Faces everywhere looking at me
But as I land on a tree I am safe from everything.

*Michael Catt  (12)*
*The Abbey School*


## THE CANDLE HOLDER

The aura of the candle,
Gives off such a wonderful scent,
It would make a perfect gift,
A glowing candle present.
The smoke from the flames are white,
No grey or dusk at all,
The flame is burning, burning,
The flame now beginning to fade.
The wax is melting fast,
Under the heat of the flame,
The warmth to comfort a poor lost child,
And give them hope again.
A shadow of shade form the holder,
A floodlight of light streaming through the stars,
light the candle again,
Make it bolder.
The flame is beginning to fade now,
The candle no longer alight,
We now return to darkness,
As the child knows that she is all right.

*Samantha Arnold  (12)*
*The Abbey School*

## THE SUN SO BRIGHT

Shining bright in the sky
Beautiful colours up so high
As bright as a burning fire
The sun rises up higher and higher
Sometimes hides away
Just like a rabbit on a winter's day.
Shining bright colours in the air.
Turning, twisting round like a baby bear.
Sun is out now it's gone
Beyond the clouds and far beyond.

*Sarah Finnis  (14)*
*The Abbey School*


## A DREAM

Fun and laughter I can hear,
All the children getting near,
But not this one, it may not seem,
Who at the moment is in a dream.

A dream of people who are good and kind,
To all little children who are left behind,
A dream that's shattered at a cry of help
The child's mum comes down to help.

To help the child she so dearly loves,
Love that I might never have,
But some day
Someone
Will love me . . . too.

*Sarah Judge  (13)*
*The Abbey School*

## THE EYES OF ANOTHER BEING

Like a shattered world
Small things become large
As I gaze into the world of spiral faces
Things change colour and their shape
One face becomes a million faces
Heaven and hell mixed together.

*Chris Laker  (12)*
*The Abbey School*


## ENDLESS THOUGHT

Glistening blond hair, sparkling red lips
A pampered face disappearing, in pale moonlight,
Soon to be an eclipse,
Face of depression was at last sight.

Soft voice, gentle feelings, deserved better than death.
Missing an endless thought, what love shall I find?
Your will to rule, encounters that of Lady Macbeth
Only this endless thought is one of a kind.

> Marble eyes, with a solid gold heart
> Flawless features, including your style
> Until death did us part
> Everyone missing the immense smile.

A sobber of sorrow, an endless thought
Strong love lasts for ever
Reasons for living, next to nought
Did I imagine this day, never.

*Andy Willis  (15)*
*The Abbey School*

# THE SKY IS FALLING DOWN

The moon and stars are falling down,
Look how they shine!
The ground is littered by the stars,
The moonlight is aqua green,
These shapes are all around!

*James Lee-Alliston  (12)*
*The Abbey School*


# DARK SHADOWS

A tree, a beautiful green tree that's a candle holder.
It has a beautiful pattern carved in the back,
When the light's right you can see the
Flickering candlelight glisten upon the wall.
A candle stands in it, shining away like
An angel, fluttering her wings,
But the fluttering's furious, roaring away
Like an angry animal.
The scent climbs its way up its ladder
And sprays into the air, swimming away happily

The centre of the candle sinks down
Forming a cave.
A cave of mysterious wonder
Smoke stirs its way up and disappears for ever.
Dark clouds form into the darkest . . .
Deepest shadows . . .

*Ashley Austen  (12)*
*The Abbey School*

## THE SHINING FUNNEL

The object is brown and black,
Carved to a cone shape,
Look through the transparent crystal,
It glows and sees everything in little squares
Made of hard firm wood like a funnel
From a science lab,
Very precious and old with a distinctive smell,
The sun shines on the crystal,
And it glows and shines,
Each square looks a different colour,
As it glimmers in the light.

*Stacia Packman  (12)*
*The Abbey School*


## LOOKING CRYSTAL

L ots of faces and objects turning round before my eyes.
O ld smells coming from the beautifully carved wood.
O utside, the base is spectacular, brown, woody and black stripes.
K eeps it safe, it's very precious.
I love the pretty glass squares and diamonds.
N icely carved and nicely shaped
G olden metal around the edge.

C one shaped, like a brown and black ice cream.
R eally interesting to look through.
Y ou'll find it very different.
S mooth, not one rough edge at all.
T urn it, nothing moves except the shapes.
A ll day you could sit and watch, watch the beautiful shapes.
L ovely crystal, real crystal.

*Lucy Beazleigh  (12)*
*The Abbey School*

## THE PRISON OF LIGHT

The prison is glowing, glowing,
A candle, that beautiful candle imprisoned,
What is its game
Though to us it is not imprisoned.

To us it casts happy, dancing shadows,
To ourselves it brings cheer to the eyes
Warmth to our hearts
It is imprisoned,
That beautiful dancer.

Dancer, oh dancer glowing dimmer
But if you look at the flame, not the stars
A new feeling, must grip your heart
That little burner in its prison of light.

See it, the little burner.
It sees you and it can see me,
All the while, that little triangle of fire
Is reduced to nothing.

It is dead.
There will be no more dancing stars
Nor bright glow.
The little burner has served its purpose.

*Michael Bedo  (12)*
*The Abbey School*

## LIGHT IN THE TREE

Tree in the night,
Oh, what a sight,
Animals dance and play,
All in the middle of May.

Each little light,
Descends from the dark,
Ready to fly away,
All in the middle of May.

The speckling bits,
In each little part,
Just like an animal heart,
Beating fast.

The light goes out,
Another one dies,
Now water is in my eyes,
The light gives out some small cries.

*Marie Ruffle  (13)*
*The Abbey School*


## CANDLE HOLDER

As the light shone upon my face,
I saw a candle holder,
Shaped like a tree it was,
I never got any colder.

The tree shaped figure,
Shone upon my wall,
It shone lots of shapes,
Like a moon that wouldn't fall.

As the candle dimmed,
Into the night,
The flame that once kept me warm,
Left me with a cold fright.

*Natasha Owen  (13)*
*The Abbey School*

# THE CANDLE'S FLAME

A light metal tree shaped candle holder,
Randomly splattered with brush strokes
Of different shades of green.
A candle layered with sheets of golden honeycomb,
Watch the shapes dance in the heart
Of the flickering flame,
The glowing light bounces off the
Tree and produces shadows.
The melting walls of the candle slowly
Melt into the rising pool of melted wax.
The wick falls into a low cowardly
Shape as the flame bends it.
As the candle burns out the spirits
Of the flame rise to the ceiling
The flame has gone but its smoky smell
And its heat still lives on.

*Elisha Hillis  (12)*
*The Abbey School*

## KALEIDOSCOPE

The kaleidoscope is round silver flashes
Like sudden flashes,
Rainbow colours everywhere,
Star shapes, hearts and lots of others,
Like little glow-worms running around,
Like fireworks in the dark sky
Simple patterns,
Fun patterns,
Light flashes, dark flashes,
The kaleidoscope is fun to use,
Shapes whizzing around.

*Jayne Rooney  (12)*
*The Abbey School*

## A WINTER'S DAY

The water from the waterfall is frozen like crystals,
Hanging on for their lives.
The fish swimming at the bottom of the pond,
The grass in the garden is green, with white patches.
But shiny as though water is washing the colours out of the ground.
Sitting in the window, watching the children playing
In the next garden,
Seeing their rosy red cheeks as they throw the cold, white snow,
When the cold weather was a distant memory,
Fish would jump right out of the water,
You could see the sun shining on their rainbow coloured scales,
As the day went on, it started getting dark and
Everyone went into play.

*Kerry Chapman  (15)*
*The Abbey School*

## PRISM

P eer through the glass and patterns you will see . . .
R ound and round lights will appear.
I nside you will find colours making different shapes
S hades of colours banding together, forming effects.
M any movements and shapes appear when looking . . .

*Krystal Trosh  (12)*
*The Abbey School*


## LOVE

Love can be what you want it to be,
It can fill you with happiness, or fill you with grief.
It can bring you out of your darkest fears,
Or break your heart, and bring you tears.

They say it's sent from God above,
If you ever fall in love.
The love sets to work and knits a snare,
And slowly spreads its bait with care.

Don't look back in the past,
And think of loves that didn't last,
If you find the right one,
And you'll be glad the love has begun.

Some people search high and low,
They don't want love to grow.
But this search should never start,
For love lives deep in the heart.

*Robert Sharp  (16)*
*The Abbey School*

## MY KNIGHT IN SHINING ARMOUR

My knight in shining armour, through the mist he came.
Sword and shield in one hand he was calling my name,
His steed was black and beautiful, shining just the same.
He came closer and closer still calling out my name.
I knew from then he was the one, the man who was in my dreams,
I knew one day we would be together, no matter how it seems.

*Tracey Court  (14)*
*The Abbey School*


## A GLOWING CANDLE

A gorgeous glowing candle
Burning on the table
Surrounded by gorgeous golden stars
Supplying beams of light
That are very bright.

A gorgeous glowing candle
Burning on the table
The shell reminds me of a bird box
Painted silver with glowing stars.

A gorgeous glowing candle
Burning on the table
With shadows of golden stars
That is gorgeous in the darkness.

*Alison Purves  (12)*
*The Abbey School*